The Ashes Quiz Book

The Ashes Quiz Book

Patrick Allen

hardie grant books
MELBOURNE · LONDON

First published in 2010 by
Hardie Grant Books (London) Limited
Dudley House
34–35 Southampton St
London WC2E 7HF
www.hardiegrant.co.uk

A copy of the British Library Cataloguing in
Publication data is available from the British Library

ISBN: 9-781-74066-976-4

Printed and bound in the EU

1 3 5 7 9 10 8 6 4 2

Contents

Introduction

Nostalgia and history are two of the great attractions of cricket, and this is sometimes forgotten in the razzamatazz of Limited Over and Twenty Twenty matches.

Although England vs Australia is not the longest series of international matches – this record is held by the United States vs Canada series that began in 1844 – it is surely the rivalry that has the most resonance with cricket followers today.

The Ashes came into being following the one-off Test at The Oval in August 1882, a match distinguished by outstanding bowling by Fred 'The Demon' Spofforth of Australia. By taking 14 wickets in the match, he was largely responsible for England being bowled out for 77, giving Australia a victory by 7 runs.

This win ranked as the first Australian victory over a full-strength English side, playing on their home turf. At the time, no one in England believed that their team could be beaten, and in the final stages of the match, one English spectator died of heart failure, and another is alleged to have bitten through his umbrella handle.

Following this sensational victory, several obituary notices were published, the most famous being the one placed by Reginald Brooks in the *Sporting Times* on 2 September 1882, which read:

In Affectionate Remembrance of ENGLISH CRICKET
Which died at The Oval on 29th August 1882
Deeply lamented by a large circle of sorrowing friends and acquaintances
R.I.P
NB The body will be cremated and the Ashes taken to Australia

In 1882–3 England, captained by The Hon. Ivo Bligh, toured Australia. On Christmas Eve, an afternoon social match was played, after which, as a joke, the wife of the host, Sir William Clarke, burnt one of the bails used in the game, putting the ashes in a small clay urn and presenting it to Bligh as a memento.

When England won the deciding Test match in Sydney after a three-match series, Bligh was presented with a velvet bag embroidered with '1883', in which to put the urn. For the past 127 years, Australia and England have continued to fight for this modest trophy, and on Bligh's death in 1927 the urn was donated to Lord's.

Over the years it is fair to say that all Australian and English cricketers alike have aspired to play in an Ashes series. This quiz book includes questions on all the great players, from W.G. Grace, Victor Trumper, Jack Hobbs, Harold Larwood and Donald Bradman, to more recent heroes such as Ian Botham, Shane Warne, Ricky Ponting and Andrew Flintoff.

There have been some Test matches since 1882–3 when Australia and England have met but the Ashes have not been at stake. These include the Triangular Series of 1912, the one-off Centenary Tests of 1977 at Melbourne and 1980 at Lord's, the Australian Bicentenary Test in 1987–8, and the series of 1979–80 which, as a three-match series, was deemed an insufficient number. For the sake of completeness I have included questions on all official Test matches between England vs Australia.

The book is divided into 10 chapters, each on a particular era or decade, with some general and trivia questions to finish. I have started with the most recent series in 2009 for some easy openers, and then head back in time, ending up with the toughest questions from the early years at the end of the 19th century.

Introduction

The questions in each section are divided into three categories:

1. SINGLES – easy runs to keep the scoreboard ticking over;
2. FOURS – more difficult, demanding more patience;
3. SIXES – very difficult, possibly requiring research and a lot of concentration.

I hope that every cricket fan will enjoy testing their knowledge of the game with this book, and even learn something new along the way.

Patrick Allen

1 The 21st Century: 2001–2009

The turn of the century saw Australian domination continuing for a further two series, though signs were emerging of a different approach by England. Their new captain was the highly competitive and 'bloody-minded' Nasser Hussain, who was to prove a worthy adversary for Australian captain Steve Waugh. Hussain became a catalyst for a new spirit of determination within the England camp and laid the seeds for the 2005 Ashes victory.

Despite the progress made by England, it was Australia who again triumphed in the 2002–3 series with Steve Waugh leading his side to a 4–1 victory. The series also marked the swansong of several legendary Australian performers including the Waugh brothers and Michael Slater, and the arrival in England colours of Steve Harmison, Marcus Trescothick and the improving Mark Butcher. But with Darren Gough, Graham Thorpe and Andrew Flintoff all missing the tour, the 'Poms' lacked the firepower necessary to break the Australian team.

In many people's eyes, 2005 was seen as the best and most competitive Ashes series since the Second World War. Under the captaincy of Michael Vaughan, who had become a world-class batsman, backed up by Thorpe and coupled with the rise of the charismatic Andrew Flintoff, England won their first Ashes series since 1986–7, despite the supreme efforts of Shane Warne, Brett Lee and Glenn McGrath. England's victory was undoubtedly aided by an injury to McGrath at Edgbaston but outrageous talent also played its part, with the debut of Kevin Pietersen, consistent runs from Andrew Strauss, Trescothick and Vaughan, all backed up by the man with the golden arm, Andrew Flintoff, and the tireless seam bowling of Matthew Hoggard.

As the new Australian captain, the prolific Ricky Ponting had a difficult act to follow in Steve Waugh. And although Matthew Hayden, Justin Langer and Adam Gilchrist all played their part, the support bowlers to Warne, Lee and McGrath were probably making one tour too many.

How it all changed in 2006–7 when Andrew Flintoff was appointed England captain to succeed Michael Vaughan, who had been sidelined by injury. The irrepressible Flintoff was reminiscent of Ian Botham at his peak, 20 years or more earlier. Like Botham, man-management was not his strongest suit, and without the discipline displayed by Atherton, Hussain or Vaughan, a 5–0 defeat gave Ponting ample revenge for 2005.

It was perhaps fitting that Australia should have bragging rights at the end of this series, which saw the retirement of so many of their truly great players including Warne, McGrath and Gilchrist, who would have been classed as all-time greats in any era of the game.

The balance of the 2009 series in England swung first one way, then the other, and after a miraculous escape in the first Test in Cardiff, England managed to win an Ashes match at Lord's for the first time in 75 years. Although the overall quality of this series in no way matched 2005, there were great individual performances from the Australians, who scored a total of eight centuries, but too often their bowlers failed to support the batsmen. For some unknown reason, the Australian selectors failed to pick a front-line spinner at The Oval, nor did they include the injury-recovered Brett Lee in the final two Tests, which certainly did not help their cause. Andrew Strauss, with his consistent batting, and Flintoff for his last 'hurrah' at Lord's, managed to see England home, despite the magnificent batting of Michael Clarke, Marcus North and Ricky Ponting.

2001–2004

SINGLES

1. Andrew Caddick made the highest score by a number 11 while batting at Edgbaston, Birmingham, in the first Test of 2001. How many runs did he make?

a) 39   b) 45   c) 49

2. Who took 3 wickets in 5 balls, in a best Test analysis of 4–42, but was also hit for 22, the highest number of runs (equal) in an over of Ashes cricket?

a) Andrew Caddick
b) Steve Harmison
c) Mark Butcher

3. What is the greatest number of runs that England has scored in the fourth innings to win a Test match against Australia in England?

a) 304   b) 315   c) 327

4. Who scored 173 not out to lead England's victory at Headingley, Leeds, in the fourth Test match of the 2001 series?

a) Mark Butcher
b) Nasser Hussain
c) Graham Thorpe

5. Which England bowler ruptured ligaments in the first innings of the first Test match of the 2002–3 series in Brisbane, and did not play again for the rest of the series?

a) Andrew Caddick
b) Steve Harmison
c) Simon Jones

6. Which player completed the first pair of his 123-Test match career in the first Test match at Brisbane on the 2002–3 tour?

7. Name the Australian who scored two centuries in an Ashes Test at Brisbane in 2002–3?

8. Who made his Australia Test debut at Melbourne in the fourth Test match of 2002–3, after an Australian record of 129 first-class matches?

a) Martin Love
b) Greg Blewett
c) Stuart Law

9. Which England batsman scored 633 runs in the Ashes series of 2002–3?

a) Nasser Hussain
b) Michael Vaughan
c) Graham Thorpe

10. Who took 10 wickets (3–121 and 7–94) in the final Test match in the 2002–3 series at Sydney, and was never picked again to play Test cricket?

a) Darren Gough
b) Angus Fraser
c) Andrew Caddick

11. Which Australian made his highest Test score of 250 at the Melbourne Boxing Day Test match in the 2000–3 series?

12. How many playing days did it take for Australia to retain the Ashes in the 2002–3 series?

    a) 9   b) 11   c) 13

13. Which batsman did Shane Warne dismiss 14 times in Ashes Test matches between 1993 and 2001?

    a) Alec Stewart
    b) Mike Atherton
    c) Graeme Hick

14. Which player scored a hundred and made five dismissals in one innings in an England vs Australia Test match in 2002–3?

15. Ten years after his England debut, which player scored his first Test century at The Oval in 2001?

16. Who began the 2001 Ashes series with consecutive scores of 152, 90 and 54?

17. Up to and including 2002–3, how many consecutive Ashes series had been won by Australia?

18. Who scored the highest innings in the 2002–3 series at Melbourne in the fourth Test?

19. Which Australian player, other than Don Bradman, was selected as one of Wisden's Five Cricketers of the Century in 2000?

20. Which Australian captain coined the term 'mental disintegration' as a reason for sledging?

FOURS

1. Where was Ricky Ponting born?

2. Who was recalled as England captain for two Tests in the 2001 series, having relinquished the role two years previously?

3. Which replacement bowler, who was called up for the third Test at Perth in 2002–3, broke down after four overs?

4. Name the player who made his debut for England at The Oval in 2001?

SIXES

1. Who became the first Pakistani-born cricketer to play for England in an Ashes Test match in the 2001 series?

2. In the second Test of the 2002–3 series in Adelaide, which bowler dismissed his brother-in-law?

See Answers on pages 117–18.

2005–2007

SINGLES

1. In the first Test of 2005, who took his 500th Test wicket at Lord's?

2. Who was the England team coach for the 2005 Ashes series?

3. Just prior to the Edgbaston Test in 2005, which bowler trod on a ball in practice and sustained a serious ankle injury?

4. Who was England's 'Man of the Match' in the second Test match at Edgbaston in 2005?

a) Andrew Flintoff
b) Marcus Trescothick
c) Michael Vaughan

5. On his Test debut at Lord's in 2005, which England player top-scored in both innings of the match?

6. In the 2005, which player – better known as a bowler – made his highest Test score in the third Test match at Old Trafford, Manchester?

7. The closest finish, in terms of runs in Ashes history, happened at Edgbaston, Birmingham, in the second Test match of 2005. Which team won, and what was the margin of victory?

8. In 2005, how many runs did Australia concede on the first day of the second Test at Edgbaston, Birmingham?

a) 307 b) 357 c) 407

9. Who was the England wicket-keeper in the 2005 Ashes winning team?

10. In 2005, who became the first overseas bowler to take 100 wickets in Test matches in England?

11. How many sixes did Andrew Flintoff hit at Edgbaston in the second Test of 2005?

12. At Old Trafford, Manchester, in the fourth Test of the 2005 series, who became the first bowler to take 600 Test wickets?

13. In the fifth Test match at The Oval in 2005, which Australian scored his first century for 14 months to save his Test-match career?

14. Which England player scored 158 in the fifth Test match at The Oval, to achieve the draw that saw England regain the Ashes in 2005?

15. In 2005, who was the winner of the Compton-Miller medal, awarded for the best player in an Ashes series?

16. Who captained England on the ill-fated 2006–7 tour of Australia?

17. Whose first delivery of the Ashes series at Brisbane in 2006–7 ended up at second slip?

18. Who was Shane Warne's 708th and last victim in Test cricket at Sydney in the fifth Test of 2006–7?

19. Who scored the second-fastest-ever Test match hundred in terms of balls received, and the fastest in England vs Australia history, at Perth in 2006–7?

20. Who was the recipient of the Compton-Miller medal following the 2006–7 series?

FOURS

1. Which England bowler took 7–109 at Adelaide in the second Test of 2006–7?

2. Which England wicket-keeper, having not scored a duck in 51 Test innings, achieved a pair at Perth on the 2006–7 tour in the second Test match?

3. Who became only the fourth spinner ever to take five wickets in an innings in Perth, on the 2006–7 series at the third Test?

4. Who, at Adelaide in the second Test match of the 2006–7 series, became only the third England player to score a double century in Australia after R.E. Foster and W.R. 'Wally' Hammond?

a) Kevin Pietersen
b) Ian Bell
c) Paul Collingwood

SIXES

1. What was the name of the substitute fielder who dismissed Ricky Ponting in the fourth Test match at Trent Bridge, Nottingham, in 2005?

2. What was the name of England's Australian bowling coach for the successful 2005 Ashes series?

See Answers on pages 118–19.

2009

SINGLES

1. In the first Ashes Test match of 2009 at Cardiff, who became the fourth batsman in Test history to score 11,000 Test runs?

2. Which two unlikely batsmen batted out the last 69 balls as the last pair, to save the first Test match for England at Cardiff in the 2009 Ashes series?

3. At Lord's in the second Test match of the 2009 series, who became the youngest England player – apart from Ian Botham – to take 50 Test wickets?

4. Before the Lord's Test match of 2009, when was the last time England beat Australia at the 'Home of Cricket'?

a) 1926   b) 1934   c) 1953

5. Which umpire stood in his 100th Test match at Lord's in 2009 and made several controversial decisions?

6. Who took his first five-wicket Ashes haul in the Lord's Test match of 2009, at the same time announcing his imminent retirement from Test cricket?

7. In the third Test of 2009, which Australian wicket-keeper made his Test debut to replace Brad Haddin at Edgbaston, Birmingham, after the toss had been made?

8. Who won the Man of the Match award in England's victory at Lord's in the 2009 series?

9. In the third Test match of 2009, who became the first right-hander to open for Australia since Michael Slater in 2001?

10. Which England bowler achieved his best Test bowling figures of 6–91 in the Australian first innings at Headingley, in the fourth Test match of 2009?

11. Who were the Men of the Series in the 2009 Ashes?

12. Which England player, making his Test debut at The Oval in the fifth Test match of the 2009 Ashes series, made a century (119)?

13. Who, at The Oval Test match of 2009, was finally dismissed for 0 following a record number of 54 innings without a duck?

14. In the fifth Test match of the 2009 series at The Oval, which bowler took 5–37, including a spell of 5–19, to undermine Australia's first innings?

15. At Headingley, in the fourth Test match of 2009, which Australian player scored his third century in six Tests?

16. Which two players had the highest aggregate of runs in the 2009 Ashes series?

17. How many centuries did Australian batsmen score in the 2009 series against England, and how many were scored by England batsmen?

18. Kevin Pietersen only played in the first two Tests of the 2009 season. Why?

19. Name the two Australians to each score two centuries in the 2009 Ashes series.

20. Who was the only batsman dismissed by Monty Panesar in the 2009 Ashes series?

FOURS

1. In the second innings of the first Test match of the 2009 series, which England player scored 74 in 83 overs?

2. What were the best bowling figures at the SWALEC Stadium, Cardiff, in the first Test match of the 2009 series?

3. Who were the three bowlers to take 20 wickets or more in the 2009 Ashes series?

4. Apart from Ricky Ponting, only one other Australian captain has lost two Test series in England. Who?

SIXES

1. Which four Australian batsmen scored centuries in the first Ashes Test of the 2009 series at Cardiff – the first time Australia had achieved this feat in an Ashes Test match?

2. Which England bowler took wickets with the first two balls of the second day's play at Edgbaston, Birmingham, in the third Test of 2009? Name the two batsmen he dismissed.

See Answers on pages 119–20.

2 Australian Supremacy: 1989–1999

The late 1980s and early 1990s had seen the creation of a bold, determined Australian team built on the hard-nosed attitude of captain Allan Border and his lieutenant, David Boon – a pugnacious batsman who still holds the record for the greatest number of lagers consumed on an Ashes-designated team-flight to London. Border had made his team not only hard to beat, but also one of the least sociable Aussie sides ever, and it's highly probable that those two qualities were synonymous.

With batsmen like Mark Taylor, Geoff Marsh and Dean Jones, backed up by bowlers such as Geoff Lawson and Craig McDermott, and players like Steve and Mark Waugh – and let's not forget Border and Boon themselves – an extremely strong side was created. They were strengthened even further in 1993 with the arrival of the greatest spinner the game has ever known, Shane Warne, followed soon after by Glenn McGrath – prince of fast–medium-pace bowlers with his relentless off-stump line, bounce and out-and-out aggression.

This formidable team was later joined by Jason Gillespie and Paul Reiffel and, towards the end of the 1990s, there was the rise of one of the finest batsmen–wicket-keepers of all time, Adam Gilchrist, whose phenomenal scoring rate added a new dimension. The 1990s had seen the rise of quick-scoring, with seemingly smaller boundaries and covered wickets leading to an increase in the number of runs scored per over. As the game became a sinecure for batsmen, bowlers had to wise-up or develop new strategies. Finger-spinners were treated with disdain and every country placed emphasis on extreme pace, bowlers of 90 mph-plus, or spinners with a 'doosra' or leg-break bowled with an off-spin action. Warne, along with Muttiah Muralitheran of Sri Lanka, Saqlain Mushtaq of Pakistan and Harbhajan Singh of India, became the yardstick by which bowlers in the future were to be judged.

The England team that ushered in the 1990s still featured Ian Botham, David Gower and Graham Gooch, but all had a lot of miles on the clock. And although Mike Atherton, Nasser Hussain, Alec Stewart and Graham Thorpe were in their early apprenticeship years in Test cricket, several of the hoped-for great talents, such as Graeme Hick and Mark Ramprakash, were destined to fall by the wayside. The bowling was in better hands with Darren Gough, Andrew Caddick, Dominic Cork and the evergreen skills of John Emburey.

When Graham Gooch retired from international cricket in 1993, Mike Atherton succeeded him as captain. Along with this honour, he had the unenviable task of rebuilding the team at a time when Australia was experiencing its longest bout of superiority since the days of Bradman. However, by 1997, England were much improved, with the burgeoning careers of Hussain and Thorpe and the early promise of slow left-arm bowler Phil Tufnell. Australia had in turn become stronger, with Steve Waugh, Shane Warne, Glenn McGrath, Michael Slater, Mark Waugh and Jason Gillespie providing a strong framework to make the team all but invincible.

1989–1991

SINGLES

1. In the first Test at Headingley in 1989, who became the first batsman to survive a sequence of 100 Test innings without a 'duck'?

   a) Graham Gooch
   b) David Gower
   c) Ian Botham

2. In 1989, who became the first captain to lead Australia to victory twice at Lord's?

3. Who, in the 1989 series, scored 393 runs before being dismissed – a record for the England vs Australia Test matches?

   a) Allan Border
   b) Steve Waugh
   c) Graham Gooch

4. When and where was the first instance of seven leg byes in an Ashes Test match?

5. Which bowler, on his debut in the Ashes series in 1989, conceded the most expensive analysis of any debutant?

   a) Angus Fraser
   b) Andrew Caddick
   c) Devon Malcolm

6. When was the only occasion that four batsmen reached 500 runs in a series in Ashes Test matches?

7. Who was the first bowler to take more than 40 wickets twice in a Test series between England and Australia?

8. Where and when did Australia achieve their hundredth Test match victory over England?

9. What is the greatest number of extras conceded by England in an Ashes Test match, and is a record for any Test in England?

a) 51 b) 61 c) 71

10. Who scored a total of 839 runs for Australia in the 1989 series – a total that has only been bettered by two other players in Ashes history?

11. On his debut, which Essex batsman opened with his county colleague Graham Gooch at The Oval in 1989 against Australia, outscored him in both innings, and never played for England again?

a) John Stephenson
b) Nick Knight
c) Paul Parker

12. Beginning in the 1989 series, whose first three centuries for Australia against England exceeded 150 and were all unbeaten?

13. In the fourth Test of the 1989 series at Old Trafford, Manchester, which wicket-keeper became only the fourth player in Test match history to score his maiden first-class century in a Test match for England?

14. Whose world-record sequence of 119 innings without a Test match duck was ended at Melbourne in the second Test match of the 1990–91 series?

15. Who scored his only Test-match hundred in Australia at Adelaide, in the fourth Test of the 1990–91 series?

16. In the second Test of the 1990–91 series, David Gower became only the second batsman after Jack Hobbs to score how many runs against Australia in Test matches?

a) 2,000   b) 2,500   c) 3,000

17. In the 1990–91 series, Steve and Mark Waugh became the first twins to play together in Test cricket. Where was the match held?

18. In the second Test match of the 1990–91 series at Melbourne, who became the first England wicket-keeper to make six dismissals in an innings against Australia?

19. Which England player, who scored 7,728 Test runs in his career, made his debut at Trent Bridge, Nottingham in the 1989 series, and was dismissed for a duck?

20. Which Australian, later to become Chairman of Selectors, played in five of the Test matches of the 1989 Ashes series?

FOURS

1. Which pair of Australian batsmen achieved the highest first-wicket partnership in Anglo–Australian Tests in the fifth Test of the 1989 series?

2. Which player scored the slowest century in England vs Australia Test matches at Sydney in the third Test match of the 1990–91 series?

3. Which Australian player, who took 291 wickets in his Test career, achieved his best analysis of 8–97 at Perth in the fifth Test of the 1990–91 series?

4. What is the second-highest number of runs scored in an Ashes series by an Australian?

SIXES

1. Name the first pair of batsmen to bat through an entire day's play in an Ashes Test match in England.

2. At Sydney in the third Test match of 1990–91, who took his first Test wicket after bowling 440 balls and conceding 191 runs?

See Answers on pages 120–21.

1993–1995

SINGLES

1. Which Surrey and England batsman made a century on his Test debut against Australia at Nottingham in 1993?

2. Who, in 1993, became the first Australian for a hundred years to make his maiden first-class century in an Ashes Test match?

3. In the Ashes Test match at Lord's in 1993, which two batsmen both made scores of 99?

4. Who in 1993, with his first delivery in an Ashes Test match against England, bowled what is frequently called 'the ball of the century' to dismiss which batsman?

5. Which wicket-keeper did not concede a bye in Australia's innings of 632–4 declared versus England at Lord's in 1993?

6. Who was Shane Warne's fellow spinner, now a Test selector, in the 1993 England vs Australia Test series?

7. Which two celebrated Australian opening batsmen were born in Wagga Wagga, New South Wales?

8. Name the Australian batsman who scored three centuries in successive Tests against England in the 1993 series.

9. Who, in 1993, scored the 100th Test century for Australia in Tests against England?

10. What is the highest number of wickets taken by a pair of Australian spinners on a tour of England? Name the players.

11. Who was the England wicket-keeper for the 1994–5 series?

12. Name the only player to be given out 'handled the ball' in an Ashes Test match.

13. At the Melbourne Test match in the 1994–5 series, who achieved the first hat-trick in an Ashes Test since 1903–4?

14. In the fifth Test of the 1994–5 series, who became the first Australian to be left on 99 not out in a Test match?

15. Which two England captains announced their retirement from international cricket prior to the fifth Test match of the 1994–5 series?

16. In the fourth Test match at Headingley in 1993, who became the first Australian to score three consecutive hundreds in a Test series against England since Don Bradman in 1938?

17. Which two players at the Headingley Test match of 1993 registered the second-highest fifth wicket partnership in Test cricket of 332 unbroken?

18. In 1993, Australia achieved a record number of centuries in a series in England. How many did they score?

19. Which batsman achieved the highest aggregate in an Ashes rubber without a hundred in the 1993 series?

a) Allan Lamb
b) Mike Atherton
c) Alec Stewart

20. Who, in the fifth Test match of the 1994–5 series, achieved his best analysis in his first-class career when he took 8–71 at Brisbane for Australia?

FOURS

1. Who was the first-ever player to be dismissed on the basis of a television replay in England, in the second Test match of the 1993 series?

2. Which Australian batsman, who later held the Test match record for the highest individual score, averaged 57.30 for a total of 1,150 runs in first-class cricket on the 1993 tour, yet failed to be selected for a single Test that year?

3. Which England off-spinner returned the best analysis on debut since 1890 in the first Test of the 1993 series at Old Trafford, Manchester?

4. In the third Test match at Sydney in 1994–5, which player was left with the highest individual score under 100 in a declared innings?

SIXES

1. Two players making their debuts in the first Test of the 1993 series – one for each side – were both born in New Zealand. Name either one.

2. In the third Test match of 1993 at Trent Bridge, which was the first pair of debutants to open England's bowling for 32 years?

See Answers on pages 121–2.

1997–1999

SINGLES

1. Which two England batsmen put on 288 for the fourth wicket in the first Test match of the 1997 series at Edgbaston?

2. Who, in the second Test match of the 1997 series at Lord's, returned the second-best analysis by any bowler in Tests at Lord's with 8–38?

3. In the 1997 series England had their lowest total at Lord's since 1888. What was it?

a) 57 b) 67 c) 77

4. At Old Trafford in the third Test match of the 1997 series, who became only the third Australian to score hundreds in both innings of a Test match?

5. Who was the first wicket-keeper to take eight catches for England in an Ashes Test match?

6. In the fourth Test at Headingley, Leeds, in 1997, who became the first batsman in England vs Australia Test matches, and only the third batsman in Test history, to be dismissed for 199?

7. Which two Australian-born brothers made their debuts for England in the fifth Test match of the 1997 series at Trent Bridge?

8. Who, in the 1997 series, broke Peter May's record of 41 Tests as the England captain?

9. Who became the first wicket-keeper to take 350 catches in Test cricket?

10. Who took 4 for 4 in 12 balls, and finished with figures of 6–60, to give England victory in the fourth Test match at Melbourne in 1998–9 by 12 runs?

11. In the second Test match of the 1998–9 series at Perth, which bowler took 4 wickets in 6 balls for Australia?

12. After being reprieved by inadequate camera positions when on 35 in the 1998–9 series, who scored 123 out of Australia's total of 184?

13. Who scored his first and only Test match hundred against Australia at Melbourne in the fourth Test match of the 1998–9 series?

 a) Mike Atherton
 b) Alec Stewart
 c) Graeme Hick

14. How many players did England select in the six-match series in 1989?

15. Which Australian-born left-arm bowler took 5–105 in his first Test match for England on the 1998–9 tour?

16. Who made 127 in his first innings against England in the 1997 series at Headingley, Leeds?

 a) Matthew Hayden
 b) Ricky Ponting
 c) Matthew Elliott

17. Name the player who kept wicket for England in the last two Test matches of the 1998–9 tour?

 a) Warren Hegg
 b) Jack Russell
 c) Paul Downton

18. Who, after 21 innings without a half-century, scored 129 in the first Test of 1997 at Edgbaston?

   a) Ian Healey
   b) Steve Waugh
   c) Mark Taylor

19. One Australian spinner took 27 wickets in the 1998–9 series. Who was he?

20. Which Australian fast bowler made his debut in Australia's losing Test match of the 1998–9 series in Melbourne, and never played Test cricket again?

FOURS

1. Name the two players who became the first pair of England bowlers to share 19 wickets in a Test match since Jim Laker and Tony Lock for England vs New Zealand at Headingley, Leeds, in 1958 (third Test)?

2. Four England players made their debut at Trent Bridge in 1993, against Australia. Name two of them.

3. Which Gloucestershire left-arm seam bowler made his debut at Headingley, Leeds, in the 1997 series, but failed to take a wicket?

4. When and where was Test cricket's longest-ever day?

SIXES

1. Which Australian, who was not part of the original 1997 touring side, was called up from Gloucestershire to play his one and only Test match at The Oval?

2. Who, when he made his debut in the third Test of the 1997 series at Old Trafford, provided the first instance of three generations of a family appearing in Test cricket?

See Answers on pages 122–3.

3 The Packer Revolution: 1977–1988

The centenary of Test cricket was marked in March 1977, at Melbourne, by a highly entertaining and competitive match. All former Ashes Test players were invited along and more than 200 ex-England players made the trip. They included Harold Larwood and Bob Wyatt from the infamous Bodyline tour; Don Bradman, Jack Fingleton, Jack Ryder and Bill O'Reilly. The main protagonists were Dennis Lillee, who at the height of his powers, took 6–26 in a match haul of 11 wickets and Derek Randall, who on his Ashes debut scored a never-to-be-forgotten 174. The net result was an Australian win by 45 runs – the same margin as in 1877.

This centenary match was probably the last cause for celebration before news broke six weeks later of Kerry Packer's World Series – initially a response to players wanting an improved split of profits that were now pouring into the game, which the Australian Cricket Board carefully husbanded. With player revolt in the air, Packer saw his chance, coupling his desire for cricket's television rights – held exclusively at the time by ABC in Australia – by setting up World Series Cricket (WSC), and at the same time to offer considerable rewards for the players. With the 1977 tour of England imminent, all but four of the selected team signed for the WSC. Morale in the Australian camp was at an all-time low, and the series was duly lost 3–0.

A new and inexperienced captain, Graham Yallop, took over for Australia in 1978–9, and England overwhelmed them 5–1, in spite of the efforts of Rodney Hogg with 41 wickets in the series. The England team, which included David Gower, Ian Botham,

31

Geoffrey Boycott and Derek Randall, under the captaincy of Mike Brearley, completely out-gunned and out-thought its opponents. However, there was one glimmer of hope for Australia in this series: the debut of Allan Border, the left-handed batsman from New South Wales, who was to have a huge impact on Australia's future.

In early 1979, peace was negotiated between the ACB and the WSC at the cost of Channel 9, the TV station owned by Packer being granted the much-coveted TV rights, and a full-strength Australian side could once again be selected. At the end of that year a three-Test match, not for The Ashes, ensued.

What can one say of 1981, 'Botham's Year'? Starting the season as captain but being replaced by Mike Brearley after the second Test match, Botham bestrode the series like a colossus with 399 runs and 34 wickets including a 50 and 149 not out, and 6–95 to win the Headingley Test match after England had followed on and Australia had failed to chase 130 in the fourth innings. In the face of adversity, Botham played one of the finest innings of all time to steal an 18-run win and turn the tide, giving a 3–1 victory in the series to England.

Allan Border, now Australian captain, was having mixed fortunes. However, backed by Geoff Lawson, a new strike bowler, he began to make his mark, with the old guard of Rodney Marsh, Rodney Hogg and Jeff Thomson providing welcome backing.

By 1985 more player problems struck, with many Australian players electing to play a rebel tour in South Africa, leading to a 3–1 margin of victory for England, in spite of 597 runs from the captain. England retained the Ashes in 1986–7 under the captaincy of Mike Gatting, with the main protagonists for England being Chris Broad with three centuries, and Botham, Emburey, Dilley and Small all contributing to a 2–1 series win.

However, the tide was turning as Allan Border's toughness started to seep through to his side, and this new hard-line approach would soon bear fruit on the 1989 tour of England.

1977–1980

SINGLES

1. Who was the last batsman to carry his bat through a Test innings in Ashes Tests?

a) Graham Gooch
b) Geoffrey Boycott
c) Chris Tavare

2. Which batsman scored a century for England in the Centenary Test between Australia and England in Melbourne in 1977?

3. Which Australian fast bowler burst onto the scene in the 1978–9 series against England and took 41 wickets – the greatest number by an Australian bowler in his home country?

4. Name the two captains in the 1980 Lord's Centenary Test between England and Australia.

5. In 1977, which batsman achieved the highest average in an England vs Australia Test series?

a) Geoffrey Boycott
b) Ian Botham
c) Graham Gooch

6. An England captain was stripped of his captaincy in 1977 because of his involvement in setting up the World Series Cricket for Kerry Packer, and was replaced by Mike Brearley. Who was he?

7. In 1977, which England fast bowler achieved the best bowling figures since Hedley Verity in 1934 in an England vs Australia Test match at Lord's?

8. What is the highest score made in a fourth innings in an England vs Australia Test match?

    a) 317   b) 357   c) 417

9. Which Australian bowler, after his first three Test matches of the 1978–9 series, had taken 27 wickets, including 5 wickets in an innings, 5 times out of 6?

10. Who, in the third Test match at Melbourne in the 1978–9 series, scored the slowest ever 3 runs in Test-match history, taking 110 minutes?

11. Which batsman was run out by Kim Hughes on 99 at Melbourne in the 1979–80 series?

12. Who was the first player in an England vs Australia Test match to use an aluminium bat?

13. Two players have batted on all five days in a Test match between England and Australia – one for England in 1977, the other for Australia in the 1980 Centenary Test. Name one of them.

14. What is the surname of the only three brothers to represent Australia in official Test matches?

15. Which Australian bowler took 11–165 (6–26 and 5–139) in the 1977 Centenary Test match in Melbourne?

16. Geoff Miller holds the record for the slowest individual innings played in an Ashes Test match, when he scored seven at Melbourne in 1978–9. How long did he take?

a) 103 minutes
b) 123 minutes
c) 143 minutes

17. In 1977, who became the first batsman to score his hundredth century in a Test match?

18. Who was the only England player to appear in both the Centenary match at Melbourne in 1976–7 and the Centenary Test match at Lord's in 1980?

19. Which future England captain made his Test debut in the third Ashes Test of 1977 at Trent Bridge?

20. Who captained Australia in the 1980 Centenary Test match at Lord's?

FOURS

1. Who scored the slowest hundred on record, in terms of balls received, in an Ashes series?

2. How many of the 1977 Australian tourists had not signed for Kerry Packer's World Series Cricket prior to the tour?

a) 7   b) 4   c) 10

3. On his debut for Australia at The Oval in the fifth Test match of 1977, who took 5–63 and scored 46, but never played another Test match?

4. Which player, on his debut for Australia in the 1977 Centenary Test at Melbourne, hit Tony Greig for five consecutive fours?

SIXES

1. Which Australian umpire, in the face of severe criticism, responded by announcing his retirement during the second Test match of the 1978–9 series?

2. Whose brainchild was the Centenary Test match between England and Australia at Melbourne in 1977?

See Answers on pages 123–4.

1981–1985

SINGLES

1. In which year did the first Test match in England include Sunday play?

a) 1981   b) 1985   c) 1989

2. Who, in Botham's match at Headingley in 1981, took 8–43 to bowl out Australia 19 runs short of victory?

3. Rodney Marsh holds the record for the greatest number of victims by a wicket-keeper in an Ashes Test series. How many did he dismiss?

a) 24   b) 28   c) 30

4. In the fourth Test match at Edgbaston in the 1981 series, Australia were set 151 to win. Who took five wickets for one run to win the match for England?

5. When was the second-ever instance in Test-match history of a team winning a Test match after following on?

6. What was unique about the England vs Australia fourth Test match at Edgbaston, Birmingham, in the 1981 series?

7. Who was the first England wicket-keeper to make 100 dismissals versus Australia?

8. In 1981, which England batsman, in the fifth Test match at Old Trafford, scored 78 runs in 423 minutes and recorded the slowest fifty in English first-class cricket at the time?
   a) Geoff Miller
   b) Paul Downton
   c) Chris Tavare

9. In the 1981 series, who scored the greatest number of sixes in a Test innings against Australia?

10. What is the slowest century recorded by an Australian in Test cricket, achieved in an Ashes Test match at Old Trafford, Manchester, in the 1981 series?

11. Who took 42 wickets in a series against England in 1981 to claim the record number of wickets in England for Australia in a series (six matches)?

12. In Ian Botham's match at Headingley against Australia in 1981, who scored 56 and put on 112 for the eighth wicket to give England a target to bowl at?

13. In an Ashes series in 1981, during the sixth Test match at The Oval, which England player took his two-hundredth wicket in the record time of 4 years, 34 days, at the age of 25?

14. At The Oval in the sixth Test of the 1981 series, who became the first Australian since 1893 to score a century on debut in England?

15. In the first Test match of the 1982–3 series at Perth, which Australian bowler dislocated his shoulder tackling a pitch invader, causing him to miss the rest of the series?

16. Which South-African-born player, who was the first to represent Australia, scored a century on his debut and set a record aggregate for Australia?

17. Who, at Adelaide in the third Test match of the 1982–3 series, became the third Australian to score 2,500 runs against England in Tests?

18. Which wicket-keeper has made the most dismissals in a series of England vs Australia Tests?

19. In the 1981 series, England played three wicket-keepers in the five Test matches. Who were they?

20. Who resigned as England captain after bagging a pair in the second Test match of the 1981 series at Lord's?

FOURS

1. Which Sussex batsman played his one and only Test match against Australia at The Oval in 1981?

2. Which former Australian fast bowler of the 1980s, nicknamed 'Henry', is now an optometrist and cricket coach?

3. Which England player took an hour to score his first run in his team's first and second innings of the 1982–3 second Test match in Perth?

4. In 1985, which England Captain scored the highest innings for England at Edgbaston, and the second-highest by an England captain after W.R. 'Wally' Hammond's 240 at Lord's in 1938?

SIXES

1. Which county cricketer for Gloucestershire was called up by Australia to play in the 1981 Ashes series?

2. Name the two Australians who bet on their team losing at Headingley in 1981, at odds of 500–1.

See Answers on pages 124–5.

1985–1988

SINGLES

1. David Gower and Graham Gooch shared a partnership of over 300 against Australia in an Ashes Test match in 1985. Where was the match played?

2. Which player has scored the most runs for England in an Ashes series in England?

a) Geoffrey Boycott
b) David Gower
c) Graham Gooch

3. On his Ashes debut in 1986–7 at Melbourne, which Barbados-born bowler took 5–48 to give England victory?

4. Which batsman, whose son is also a current Test-match cricketer, scored three Test-match centuries for England vs Australia in the 1986–7 series?

5. Name the England wicket-keeper who scored a century in the 1986–7 Test match in Perth.

6. The tallest player to play in England vs Australia Test matches made his debut in the first Test of the 1986–7 series at Brisbane. Who was he?

7. Who, in the first Test match of the 1985 series at Headingley, took 3 wickets in 4 balls, and was only the second English bowler to achieve this feat?

8. Which Australian fast bowler had the nickname 'Fruitfly', due to his reputation as the biggest Australian pest (he also had a moustache)?

9. In the second Test match of the 1985 series, who recorded the highest score by an Australian captain at Lord's?

10. In a Test match in Australia, which England batsman smashed the stumps down with his bat after being bowled for 139?

11. Which Australian leg-spinner scored five consecutive Test match 'ducks' in 1985?

12. Who achieved the greatest number of runs scored in an over by an England batsman?

13. In the third Test at Headingley in 1981, which wicket-keeper surpassed J.T. Murray's total of 1,270 catches in first-class cricket?

14. At Old Trafford in the fourth Test match of the 1985 series, who became the youngest Australian to take eight wickets in a Test innings?

a) Geoff Lawson
b) Merv Hughes
c) Craig McDermott

15. In the sixth Test match of the 1985 Ashes series, which player was only declared fit on the morning of the match, having twisted his left knee two days before?

16. Which two players, in the fifth Test match at Edgbaston in 1985, achieved the second highest partnership for any wicket against Australia at the time?

17. In the second Test match of the 1986–7 series at Perth, who emulated Garry Sobers in achieving the Test treble of 1,000 runs, 100 wickets and 100 catches?

18. In the second Test match in Perth, on the 1986–7 tour of Australia, who became only the third wicket-keeper, after Les Ames and Alan Knott, to score a century against Australia?

19. Who, on his maiden tour of Australia, became only the fourth England captain in the 20th century to successfully defend the Ashes abroad after Percy Chapman, Len Hutton and Mike Brearley?

20. Which England batsman scored 732 runs in the 1985 series against Australia?

FOURS

1. Which England player, now a first-class umpire, scored 175 in his first Test match against Australia at Headingley in 1985?

2. Which former Manchester United footballer made his one and only Test appearance against Australia at Trent Bridge, Nottingham, in the third Test match of 1985? His son later played for England.

3. In the Lord's Text match of 1985, which 38-year-old Australian leg-spinner took 5–68?

4. Who was so unknown when selected to play for Australia in the 1986–7 series, it was assumed the selectors had chosen the wrong player?

SIXES

1. Which player, later to become a Test match selector, played once for England in an Ashes Test match at Adelaide in 1986–7, and was never selected again?

2. Who was the fourth-youngest England player to play a Test match versus Australia, and the first from Dominica?

See Answers on pages 125–6.

4 The Post-War Years: 1950–1975

Although 1950–51 was the second tour to Australia since the Second World War, the shortages, rationing and general exhaustion of Britain seemed emphasized by a highly motivated and good-quality Australian team who had absorbed the retirement of Donald Bradman. Left with the incomparable pair of Lindwall and Miller as the main pace attack, the dazzling and dapper left-hander Neil Harvey, Lindsay Hassett and Arthur Morris leading the batting, and a series of first-rate all-rounders, Australia seemed stronger than ever. Eighteen years after his last tour to Australia, England's captain was Freddie Brown, now aged 39. The line-up of his team looked more than competitive, with Len Hutton, Denis Compton, Cyril Washbrook, Godfrey Evans and Trevor Bailey. But few of the supporting cast rose to the occasion, Compton enduring one of the worst series of his career, although Alec Bedser did take 30 wickets.

The Australian surprise packet was the spinner Jack Iverson, who bowled off-spin with a leg-break action and took 27 wickets. Len Hutton batted extremely well throughout the series, but it was not until the fifth Test that England achieved a victory, Bedser taking 10 wickets, and Reg Simpson scoring a magnificent century to end an Australian run of 26 Tests unbeaten. It was too late to save the series, however, with Australia winning 4–1.

By 1953, the year of the Coronation, England finally recovered the Ashes at The Oval, winning the series 1–0. Australia had turned to youth under Lindsay Hassett, with the emergence of Jimmy Burke, Colin McDonald and Richie Benaud. This series was dominated by

Bedser's 39 wickets, backed up by Trevor Bailey and Willie Watson's heroic match-saving partnership at Lord's, and several fluent innings from captain Len Hutton – the first professional to hold the role of captain since the 1880s – and Peter May.

The 1954–5 tour saw a catastrophic first-Test defeat at Brisbane on a rain-affected wicket, but the England team, led by Hutton, turned the tables as a result of great bowling by Frank Tyson. Hutton, supported by Brian Stratham and Peter Loader and Bill Edrich, Colin Cowdrey and Peter May providing the runs, England ran out series winners, 3–1.

Laker's year followed in 1956 when his 46 wickets almost single-handedly consigned Australia to another 3–1 drubbing. In an extremely wet summer, a strong Australian batting side supported by quality all-rounders such as Miller, Lindwall, Benaud and Alan Davidson was no match for a supreme off-spinner, who was in the form of his life.

The 1958–9 series was much more successful for Australia, who cruised to a 4–0 win, slightly tainted by the throwing controversy – the main culprit being Australia's Ian Meckiff. The rise of Norman O'Neill, together with outstanding performances from Colin McDonald and Richie Benaud, the new captain, completely eclipsed an underpowered England batting line-up, redeemed only by the efforts of Cowdrey and May.

With Benaud as captain, new blood was brought in for the 1961 series, including the openers Bill Lawry and Bobby Simpson, and the result was a 2–1 margin of victory for Australia. The main players for England were May, Ted Dexter, Ken Barrington, Brian Statham and Fred Trueman, with the series turning on a sensational match at Old Trafford, with Benaud bowling Australia to unexpected victory.

Ted Dexter's side of 1962–3 featured outstanding performances from Barrington and Cowdrey as well as the captain, but a 1–1 series draw proved it was a batmen's series, with Simpson, Lawry, Harvey and O'Neill matching their efforts for Australia.

The Australian captaincy was passed to Bobby Simpson in 1964, and ended in a 1–0 result in his favour. The series was notable for the debut of Geoffrey Boycott for England, and for some high scoring by Simpson, Bill Lawry, Ted Dexter and Ken Barrington. The only positive result was achieved at Headingley due to a great innings from the previously out-of-form Peter Burge. Bowlers Graham McKenzie and Neil Hawke made their mark, while Fred Trueman, in his last Ashes series, became the first bowler to take 300 Test wickets.

The 1965–6 series saw the arrival of Australian batsman Doug Walters, with centuries in his first two Tests, and a glut of runs from both teams. Another drawn series followed in 1968, with England winning a dramatic Oval Test after the ground was flooded, and Derek Underwood taking 7–50, once the crowd had mopped up the outfield. One all-time great making his Ashes debut in this series was John Snow, who went on to have his best-ever series in Australia in 1970–71, when Ray Illingworth's side beat Australia 2–0.

The 1972 series also ended in a draw. Bob Massie took 16 wickets for Australia at Lord's – a never-to-be-repeated performance from him. Australia had Dennis Lillee, arriving in his pomp, with Rodney Marsh, Greg and Ian Chappell and Ross Edwards providing the runs. John Snow continued to be the stand-out English fast bowler, with Boycott and Edrich also having good series.

Again the wheel was turning with Lillee and a new whirlwind, Jeff Thomson. Thomson's arrival heralded the most terrifying Test bowling attack, with Dennis Lillee brushing aside Mike Denness' shell-shocked side 4–1, and between them taking 58 wickets. Although England had Derek Underwood, their batting, aside from Edrich, lacked consistency and the tenacity to cope with such an intimidating assault.

1950–1956

SINGLES

1. Who was the Australian captain when England won back the Ashes in 1953?

2. Which player has taken the greatest number of wickets in an England vs Australia Test series?

3. Who were the two batsmen who saved the 1953 Lord's Test match against Australia?

4. Name the only Australian not dismissed by Jim Laker when he took 19 wickets for England vs Australia at Old Trafford in 1956.

5. In Laker's match at Old Trafford in 1956, which bowler took the twentieth wicket for England?

6. Three batsmen were recalled to play for England in the 1956 series versus Australia. Name one of them.

7. Which celebrated England batsman managed only 53 runs in eight innings in the 1950–51 Ashes series?

8. From which end of the ground at Old Trafford, Manchester, in 1956 was Jim Laker bowling when he achieved his match analysis of 19–90 (9–37 and 10–53)?

9. In 1956, where did Keith Miller take 10 wickets in a Test match for the only time in his 55 Test-match career?

10. Which series featured, for the first time, complete covering of the pitches for England vs Australia Test matches in Australia?

11. Who became the first captain to win an Ashes rubber after losing the toss in all five Tests?

12. In the fifth Test at Sydney in 1954–5, which player allowed himself to be bowled by Ray Lindwall, enabling Lindwall to achieve a total of 100 wickets in Australia vs England Tests?

13. Which batsman was dismissed twice by Jim Laker in one day for a pair at Old Trafford, Manchester, in 1956?

14. Name the player who held five catches off Laker's bowling in the Old Trafford Test match of 1956.

15. Which player was caught by the wicket-keeper in all eight of his innings in the 1956 Ashes series?

16. Which English bowler dismissed an Australian batsman 18 times in 20 Test matches? Name the batsman.

17. Who captained England at Melbourne in 1950–51, and ended a record run of 25 consecutive matches without defeat by Australia (20 wins and 5 draws)?

18. Which England player made the first of his six successive tours to Australia in 1954–5?

19. Who captained the Australian team on the tour of 1956?

20. Which celebrated player, who was also an England soccer international, made a century on his Ashes debut for England in 1953?

FOURS

1. Who was the first batsman to score a 50 in each innings of his first England vs Australia Test, without reaching a hundred in either of them?

2. Which pair of England bowlers took 46 wickets between them in the 1954–5 series?

3. Which mystery spinner, who played in only five Test matches in his career, took 21 wickets in the 1950–51 series to give Australia a series victory?

4. Who carried their bat for 156 not out in a total 272 for England at Adelaide in the fourth Test of the 1950–51 series?

SIXES

1. What was the name of the Melbourne groundsman who illegally watered the MCG wicket during the third Test match of the 1954–5 series?

2. In the 1953 series, who eclipsed Maurice Tate's record of 38 wickets in a series before being overtaken by Jim Laker in 1956?

See Answers on page 127.

1958–1966

SINGLES

1. In spite of playing 79 Test matches, who captained Australia only once, in 1961 at Lord's, when Richie Benaud injured his shoulder?

    a) Neil Harvey
    b) Peter Burge
    c) Alan Davidson

2. Which England batsman scored a century in both his first and last Test matches against Australia?

    a) Raman Subbe Row
    b) Geoff Pullar
    c) Bob Barber

3. In 1958–9, during the second Test match at Melbourne, who scored the first century by an England captain in Australia since the 1901–2 series?

4. Where was the first televised Ashes Test match in Australia held?

5. What is the fewest number of runs scored in one day in an Ashes Test match?

6. Who hit the only 6 in the 1958–9 series?

    a) Ted Dexter
    b) Peter May
    c) Fred Trueman

7. Whose innings of 160 enabled Australia to retain the Ashes in the 1964 series at Headingley, in the third Test match?

a) Bill Lawry
b) Peter Burge
c) Norman O'Neill

8. Which batsman scored the only triple hundred in a home Test match for Australia?

a) Bob Cowper
b) Bobby Simpson
c) Norman O'Neill

9. In 1964, who bowled the greatest number of consecutive overs in an Ashes Test match?

10. When Freddie Trueman took his 300th wicket in his Test-match career at The Oval in 1964 against Australia, who was the catcher?

11. Name the two England off-spinners who bowled in tandem during the 1965–6 series.

12. Who bowled the greatest number of balls in an innings in an Ashes Test match?

13. Name the only Test match in which both sides totalled over 600 in their first innings.

14. Which batsman scored the slowest ever 50 for Australia in an Ashes match?

15. Which Australian player did not score a century until his thirtieth Test match, and then went on to make it a triple?

16. What is the highest score by an England batsman on the first day of a Test match against Australia?

17. Which batsman, in the 1965–6 series, scored back-to-back centuries in his first two Tests?

18. On which tour did Australia lose one Test match by an innings, then win the next by an innings – the first time this had happened in consecutive Tests?

19. Which England batsman scored a century in 122 balls at Melbourne in the fifth Test of 1965–6, reaching his 100 with a 6?

20. Which celebrated English fast bowler took 11–88 (5–58 and 6–30) in the third Test at Headingley in 1961?

FOURS

1. Before Peter May scored 113 at Melbourne in the second Test match of 1958–9, who was the last England captain to score a Test match century against Australia?

2. What was the name of the tour manager of the 1962–3 England tour of Australia?

3. Who bowled the England captain Peter May for a duck in the second innings of the fourth Test at Old Trafford in 1961, precipitating a sensational victory for Australia?

4. Which celebrated English left-hander hit a century on his Ashes debut at Lord's in 1964, and went on to score seven centuries and 2,644 runs against Australia?

SIXES

1. Who scored the first century for Australia in four years and 11 Test matches during the second Test match of the 1958–9 series at Melbourne?

2. Which Australian bowler played only five Test matches – all on the 1964 tour – but dismissed Geoffrey Boycott in his first three Test innings?

See Answers on pages 128–9.

1968–1975

SINGLES

1. Which England captain, in the 1974–75 series in Australia, stood down as a player due to his lack of form?

2. Which player has taken the greatest number of wickets in an England vs Australia Test series?

3. Which two brothers each scored centuries for Australia vs England at The Oval in 1972, during the fifth Test?

4. Who was Geoffrey Boycott's opening partner on his Test debut against Australia in 1964, and was far better known as an off-spinner?

5. In the 1964 Old Trafford Test match between England and Australia, which two batsmen scored 311 and 256 respectively?

6. In the 1975 series against Australia, which England cricketer averaged over 60 with the bat, and took a wicket in his first over in Test cricket?

7. On his first appearance in an Ashes Test in 1972, who took 16 wickets in a Test match against England at Lord's?

8. Where in England was an Ashes Test match abandoned due to vandalism?

9. Who made his debut for England in the fourth Test of the series against Australia in 1970–71 at Sydney, having flown out as a replacement for Alan Ward?

    a) R.G.D. 'Bob' Willis
    b) Ken Shuttleworth
    c) Peter Lever

10. Who is the only cricketer to score an Ashes double century at the Gabba?

    a) Bill Lawry
    b) Keith Stackpole
    c) Bobby Simpson

11. At which English Test match ground was Fusarium Patch Disease blamed for a sub-standard wicket for an England vs Australia Test match?

12. At Edgbaston in 1975, who bagged a pair in his first Test match against Australia?

13. Who holds the record for the most catches by a fielder in an England vs Australia Test match?

14. Which batsman, at Perth in the 1974–5 series, scored 100 runs in a session between tea and close of play on the second day?

a) Doug Walters
b) Paul Sheahan
c) Keith Stackpole

15. In 1974–5, who scored the first century at Brisbane in an Ashes Test since the 1936–7 series for England?

16. What is the record number of dismissals by an England wicket-keeper in a series against Australia?

17. Which South African-born player scored 158 for England in the final Test match at The Oval in 1968 against Australia, causing a political crisis and ultimately the exclusion of South Africa from Test cricket?

18. Which celebrated batsman captained England for the first and only time at Headingley in 1968, when Colin Cowdrey was injured?

19. Which England captain led his team from the field of play in a deciding Ashes Test match in Australia?

20. Who was Chairman of the Australian Selectors for the 1970–71 series?

FOURS

1. Which two Australian bowlers, in the 1970–71 series, were termed 'the most insipid new-ball pairing in Ashes history'?

2. Name the bowler who, in taking 31 wickets in the 1970–71 series, dismissed 24 batsmen from the top-order.

3. In the sixth Test match of the 1970–71 tour, which player was brought in to replace Bill Lawry as opening batsman?

4. In 1970–71, how many Australian players were given out lbw?

SIXES

1. Which batsman scored the highest individual score for England in the Ashes series of 1972, and what was it?

2. At Headingley in 1968, who were the two substitute captains that captained their only Test matches in an England vs Australia series?

See Answers on pages 129–30.

5 The Bradman Era: 1930–1948

Although Don Bradman had made his promising Ashes debut in the 1928–9 series, the staggering impression he made in England in 1930 – when he scored a total of 974 runs – eclipsed all Test series batting records against a strong English team. He established a dominance maintained for almost two decades and, had the Second World War not intervened, his record may have been even greater. Alongside Bradman were Bill Ponsford, Bill Woodfull, Stan McCabe, Archie Jackson, Bill O'Reilly, Clarrie Grimmett and Bert Oldfield, and a 2–1 series victory ensued, despite England boasting batsmen of the calibre of Sutcliffe, Hammond and Duleepsinhji.

The sheer phenomenon of Bradman pushed the England team into devising a tactic to combat this extraordinary run machine. Following a period of rain-affected play in The Oval Test of 1930, it was rumoured that Bradman was having difficulties with short-pitched deliveries, and he was indeed hit on the chest by Harold Larwood. In light of this, Douglas Jardine and the former England and Nottinghamshire captain, Arthur Carr, hatched the idea of fast leg theory, later to be termed 'Bodyline', that was to sour relations between England and Australia when put into practice on the 1932–3 tour. With a quartet of pace bowlers consisting of Larwood, Voce, Bowes and Gubby Allen, the plan was to have seven or eight fielders on the leg-side in close-catching positions. Although Bradman missed the first Test, a brilliant counter-attack by Stan McCabe, with an unbeaten 187, showed leg theory could be dominated. In spite of this, however, and with Larwood taking 10 wickets in the match, Australia was beaten conclusively.

With the return of Bradman for the second Test, Australia, with three spinners in their side, led by Bill O'Reilly, won a relatively low-scoring game before the third Test at Adelaide – one of the most controversial and contentious matches of all time. This match saw Jardine intensifying his Bodyline attack, resulting in Oldfield suffering a fractured skull and Woodfull being hit over the heart. Following England's victory, cables were exchanged between the Australian Board of Control and MCC, claiming 'Bodyline' tactics unsportsmanlike and causing concern about future Anglo–Australian relations.

With Australia losing at Adelaide as well as the next two matches, England won the series 4–1. Bradman still scored a total of almost 400 runs, but 'Bodyline' finally proved he was mortal. The long-term consequences for the architects of leg theory – Larwood, who took 33 wickets in the series, and Jardine, the captain who instructed his players to bowl 'Bodyline' – were severe. Larwood never played Test cricket again, and Jardine was unceremoniously dumped as captain in 1933 after the establishment turned against him: leg theory was not, however, to be legislated against for another 20 years, when leg-side fielding limits were imposed.

The 1934 series was much less controversial: Bradman and Ponsford led the batting, with Grimmett and O'Reilly taking 53 wickets between them in a 2–1 series defeat for England, only relieved by a win at Lord's.

The Test series of 1936–7 was almost a goodwill tour led by Gubby Allen, who had refused to bowl leg theory on the previous tour. The series was won by Australia, 3–2, after being two matches down. With Bradman being made captain of Australia, a cordial relationship between Allen and Bradman did much to make the tour a success. The Ashes series of the 1930s – apart from 1932–3 – had seen Bradman rack up 974, 758 and 810 runs, and although he had a leaner year in 1938 – with one Test abandoned, and being unable to bat at The Oval due to an ankle injury – he still made a century in each of the Tests in which he batted. The great event of 1938, however, was the 364 scored by Len Hutton at The Oval to eclipse Bradman's 334 at Leeds in 1930, which was the highest individual score for Australia against England. Hutton's monumental effort in a total of 903–7 declared at The Oval was the highest Test-match innings, until beaten by Garry Sobers in 1958, and has remained England's highest individual Test innings for more than 60 years.

Eight years were to elapse, with the Second World War preventing another Ashes series until 1946–7, and with Bradman struggling before the five-Test series began, there was some doubt about his form and fitness. Normal service was, however, resumed, and Bradman made 187 in the first Test at Brisbane after surviving a clear catch in the slips on 28, which the umpire turned down (much to the chagrin of his opposite number W.R. 'Wally' Hammond, the England captain). It is on such incidents that cricket history changes, and had Bradman been dismissed, he may have chosen to retire, particularly when later in the series, at Sydney, he was caught at short-leg on 22 and went on to make 234 following another umpiring error. A 3–0 series victory for Australia ensued, and a number of new faces, who went on to become Test greats, made their debuts. These included Arthur Morris, Keith Miller, Ray Lindwall, Don Tallon and Bill Johnson, whilst for England, Alec Bedser had his first taste of Test cricket.

Bradman's farewell tour of 1948, at the age of 40, was with one of the finest teams ever to tour England – they became known as 'The Invincibles'. Neil Harvey further strengthened the batting, and Australia demolished England 4–0. The highlight was the last day of the fourth Test: a run-chase to reach a target of 404 at Headingley, resulted in a win by seven wickets with 'The Don' scoring 173 not out. His final poignant farewell to Ashes Tests, however, was his second ball 'duck' at The Oval when bowled by Eric Hollies, who thus deprived him of a Test career average of over 100.

In the history of the game, there has been no batsman of greater achievement or quality as Bradman. His dominant role as player, captain and selector – albeit controversial at times – has overall helped place Australia in its pre-eminent position for the final 70 years of the 20th century.

1930–1933

SINGLES

1. What is the highest score ever made by a nightwatchman in an Ashes Test match?

2. Don Bradman holds the record for the greatest number of runs in a day in an Ashes Test. How many did he score?

3. Which Australian wicket-keeper suffered a fractured skull during the third Test match at Adelaide on the 1932–3 Bodyline tour?

4. Name the English batsman who averaged 84.42 per innings in his seven appearances in Ashes Test matches – the highest by an English batsman.

5. An Australian fast bowler made his debut in the Bodyline series when, for the last Test, he was called in to try to emulate the England fast-bowling attack. Who was he?

6. Who were the two Nottinghamshire teammates who opened the bowling for England in the 1932–3 Bodyline tour of Australia?

7. In the first Test of the Bodyline series at Sydney in 1932–3, who dismissed Bradman's first ball, taking his only Test wicket in Australia?

8. Who is the oldest player ever to compete in an Ashes Test match?

9. What was the highest innings score ever made at Lord's, achieved in the second Test match of 1930?

10. In 1930, who became the first Australian captain to score a Test century in England since George (G.H.S.) Trott in 1896?

11. Who is the only player to have scored three double hundreds in an Ashes Test series in an aggregate of 974 and an average of 139.14 per innings?

12. Who was the England vice-captain for the 1932–3 Bodyline tour?

13. What is the fastest double hundred (in minutes) scored in an England vs Australia Test match?

14. In the infamous Bodyline series match at Adelaide in 1932–3, which player carried his bat through Australia's second innings?

15. What was the first Test match in an Ashes series where England failed to include a specialist slow bowler?

16. In the 1930 series, who reached 1000 runs in Ashes Tests during his seventh Test and thirteenth innings?

17. Which player was dismissed at Lord's in 1930 shortly after scoring his only Test hundred against Australia and accidentally swallowing a bluebottle fly?

18. Who was the England manager for the 1932–3 tour of Australia?

19. What was England's lowest score in the Bodyline series?

a) 156 b) 139 c) 144

20. Who played his last match for England in the fifth and final Test of the 1932–3 series?

FOURS

1. What is the record partnership for any wicket in England vs Australia Test match history, and who were the batsmen involved?

2. In the first Test match of the 1932–3 series at the Sydney Cricket Ground, who emulated Ranjitsinhji and Duleepsinhji by becoming the third Indian Prince to score a hundred in his first Test match against Australia?

3. In which Ashes Test match did both captains make centuries for the first time?

4. Which journalist created the term 'Bodyline'?

SIXES

1. Who dismissed Stan McCabe with a sensational catch as a substitute fielder at Trent Bridge, Nottingham, during the first Test match of the 1930 series, although he only played one first-class match in his career?

2. Which much-loved and celebrated Australian batsman died at the age of 23, in Brisbane, on the same day that England won the Bodyline series at The Gabba?

See Answers on pages 130–31.

1934–1938

SINGLES

1. What is the record margin of victory in all Test cricket, achieved by England in the 1938 Oval Test match?

2. In 1938, who played the longest innings by any batsman in an Ashes Test, staying at the crease for 13 hours and 17 minutes?

3. What is the highest partnership by England in Test matches against Australia?

4. Name Australia's only victory between 1928 and 1938 to which Don Bradman did not contribute a century.

5. Who was the first batsman to miss a century by 1 on his Test debut, when he was dismissed for 99?

6. In 1934, who captained England in his first Test match against Australia?

7. Who took 15–104 for England vs Australia at Lord's in 1934?

8. Who was the only Australian batsman to exceed 500 runs on the 1938 series in England?

9. What is the record number of byes conceded in a Test innings in an Ashes Test match?

a) 33　　　　　　b) 37　　　　　　c) 43

10. England defeated Australia at Lord's in 1934. When was their previous win in an Ashes Test match at Lord's?

11. Who was the first player to achieve the wicket-keeper's double of 100 victims and 1,000 runs?

12. When was the only occasion that four batsmen have scored hundreds in the same innings of a match, out of a total of seven centuries (a record) scored in the match?

13. At the age of 20 years and 19 days, who is the youngest-ever century maker in an Ashes Test match for England?

14. Which player, having scored four hundreds in successive Test innings – the first batsman to do so – was out first ball in his next innings at Brisbane in 1936–7?

15. In the Lord's Test of 1938, which Australian batsman scored a double century, and in so doing became the first man to ever score a double century and carry his bat through an innings?

16. What is the greatest number of runs scored in a day's play in an England vs Australia Test match?

a) 425　　　　　　b) 450　　　　　　c) 475

17. Which Australian bowler took 102 wickets against England in 19 Test matches, and a total of 144 in 27 Tests against all countries at 22.59?

18. Who was the second-highest scorer after Len Hutton's 364 in England's record total of 903–7 at The Oval in 1938?

19. Who was the batsman who scored 240 at Lord's in 1938 against Australia?

20. In 1934, which player reached 1,000 Test runs in the shortest time?

FOURS

1. Which batsman has come closest to scoring a century before lunch in an Ashes Test match for England on the first day?

2. What is the highest partnership in England vs Australia Test matches, and who were the two batsmen involved?

3. In the 1936–7 series, who bowled what was described as the 'ball of the century' at Adelaide, and to whom?

4. Which celebrated Australian Rules footballer was selected to play as a fast bowler in the 1936–7 series, and was accused of bowling 'Bodyline' in a Sheffield Shield match earlier in that season?

SIXES

1. What is the highest total through which a batsman has carried his bat in a Test match, and who was the batsman? This is both an Ashes and an all-Tests record.

2. At The Oval in 1934, who made the last Test appearance in an Ashes Test match by a pre-1914 Test player?

See Answers on pages 131–2.

1946–1948

SINGLES

1. Who dismissed Don Bradman for a duck in his last Test innings at The Oval in 1948?

2. In 1946–7, on which ground did Australia achieve its biggest victory by an innings against England?

3. Who, playing in his first Test match against Australia, conceded no byes in a total of 659?

4. In the first post-war Test match between Australia and England at Brisbane in 1946–7, which batsman was given not out on 28 and went on to score 187?

5. And who took the catch?

6. When was the first occasion that a batsman on each side scored hundreds in each innings?

7. Who was the first Australian left-hander to score a hundred in his debut Test against England, and when did he accomplish this feat?

8. When was the first drawn Test match in the Ashes series in Australia after 1881–2?

9. Who was the first England player to score 50 in each innings and take 5 wickets in the same Test?

10. On Don Bradman's last tour of England in 1948, who was the England captain for all five Test matches?

11. How many consecutive Tests against England did Bradman score at least one 50, with this run coming to an end in the third Test of the 1948 series?

   a) 12   b) 14   c) 16

12. Godfrey Evans holds the overall record for remaining scoreless in an Ashes Test match – a world record for all first-class cricket. How long was he without a run?

13. In 1948, Australia achieved the highest score in a fourth innings to win an Ashes Test match. How many did they score?

14. Who was the last England cricketer, before Graham Gooch in 1975, to wear a moustache?

15. Which Australia Test player, on the 1948 tour by 'The Invincibles', later played county cricket for Somerset?

16. Five members of Don Bradman's Invincibles team were made Wisden Cricketers of the Year in 1949. Name two of them.

17. How many Test centuries did Don Bradman score at the MCG?

18. Two players scored 234 in an Ashes Test match in 1946–7. S.G. 'Sid' Barnes was one. Who was the other?

19. Which well-known bowler toured Australia on three occasions in 1932–3, 1936–7 and 1946–7, playing 11 Tests, but never played a home Test against Australia?

20. Name the England bowler who dismissed Arthur Morris 18 times in 20 Test matches, and dismissed Don Bradman five times in successive innings.

FOURS

1. When were the two occasions on which Don Bradman scored a century and a duck in the same match against England?

2. Which Australian bowler took 6–20 at The Oval in 1948 when England was dismissed for 52?

3. Which Australian Test cricketer, who played in the 1946–7 series, later played county cricket for Nottinghamshire, and twice achieved the double of 1,000 runs and 100 wickets in a season?

4. Which celebrated Australian cricketer wrote *The Art of Cricket*?

SIXES

1. Who was the only other Australian, aside from Don Bradman, to make more than 500 runs on the 1948 Tour?

2. Which Australian bowler took more than 25 wickets in the Bodyline series of 1932–3?

See Answers on pages 132–3.

6 The Roaring Twenties: 1920–1929

Following the First World War, the 1920–21 series saw some major names make the transition to Test cricket. Foremost among the Australian team was the all-rounder Jack Gregory, whose express bowling, dynamic fielding and explosive batting had come to the fore when the Australian Imperial Forces side had toured England in 1919. Several other members of this team – Herbie Collins, Johnny Taylor, 'Nip' Pellew and Charlie Kelleway – were also to wear the 'baggy green'. With the leg-spinner Arthur Mailey, combined with Ted McDonald as Jack Gregory's new-ball partner, Australia were formidable opponents. Although England still had Jack Hobbs, Patsy Hendren, Frank Woolley and Wilfred Rhodes under the captaincy of Johnny Douglas, they were no match for a rampant Australian side who captured the series with a 5–0 whitewash, and followed this with a 3–0 drubbing of England in 1921, both under the captaincy of Warwick Armstrong.

In 1924–5, the English openers Hobbs and Sutcliffe began their alliance at the top of the order. The former, though aged 42, still scored three centuries in the series, and with Maurice Tate taking 38 wickets, a better result than a 4–1 defeat really should have been achieved. This series saw Australia debut 32-year-old New Zealand-born leg-spinner Clarrie Grimmett who, following 11 wickets for Australia in his first game, was to be ever-present until the 1934 series, taking 216 wickets in his Test career.

Following three rather harrowing post-war series, England finally won back the Ashes in 1926 under the leadership of Percy Chapman, albeit 1–0 with four draws. Australia, led by Herbie

Collins, had Charlie Macartney, who scored three centuries in the series. Newcomers Bill Woodfull and Bert Oldfield made their mark, as did Harold Larwood for England who, with Hobbs, Sutcliffe and Wilfred Rhodes, were good value for their win.

Blood-letting by the Australian selectors followed this Ashes defeat and the 1928–9 series saw the debut of Donald Bradman and Archie Jackson, who had a short but glittering career before his premature death aged 23. In a high-scoring series – with Hammond amassing 905 runs, coupled with Hobbs and Sutcliffe as an opening partnership – England ran out comfortable victors by 4–1. This was to prove the lull before the whirlwind that was Don Bradman.

1920–1923

SINGLES

1. Which player captained his country in the greatest number of Tests without defeat?

2. What is the greatest number of wickets taken by an Australian in an innings of an Ashes Test match?

3. Which England Test captain won an Olympic Boxing Gold Medal in the 1908 Olympics when he beat the Australian opponent Snowy Baker?

4. Which fielder has taken the greatest number of catches in an Ashes series?

5. How many players did England use in the 1921 Test match against Australia?

   a) 25   b) 30   c) 35

6. Who is the oldest player to make a maiden Test match 100 in an Ashes Test?

7. Who was the victorious captain in the first-ever 'whitewash' (5–0) victory in an Ashes series?

8. Which player was the first to score two 90s in a match for England?

   a) Frank Woolley
   b) Patsy Hendren
   c) George Brown

9. Who bowled two consecutive overs in an Ashes Test match?

   a) Jack Gregory
   b) Arthur Mailey
   c) Warwick Armstrong

10. Who top-scored in the first innings of his only Test match against Australia?

11. Which Australian batsman of the 1920s was nicknamed 'The Governor General'?

12. Which Australian captain left his team to organize themselves, fielded in the deep and picked up a stray newspaper 'to see who we're playing'?

13. In the 1920–21 series, which player took 23 wickets, averaged over 70 with the bat, and also took 15 catches?

14. Who was the first bowler to concede 300 runs in a Test match?

15. In 1920–21, which Australian player scored 552 runs in the series, following his outstanding tour to England with the AIF team in 1919?

16. Sir Pelham Walker founded which magazine in 1921?

17. In 1922, which Australian opening batsman later partnered Jack Gregory as an opening bowler, following the decision of Ted MacDonald to become a professional in England?

18. What is the record aggregate of runs for an England vs Australia Test match and when was it achieved?

19. Which celebrated Australian leg-spinner of the 1920s, who also happened to be a gifted artist, wrote an autobiography entitled *10 for 66 and All That*?

20. Who was the first player to score 2,000 runs and take 100 wickets in Test cricket?

FOURS

1. Which batsman is said to have inspired Don Bradman's ambition to play for Australia, after he saw him score 170 in the fifth Test of the 1920–21 series in Sydney?

2. Who is the oldest Australian to score a century on his Ashes debut?

3. Name the player who has appeared in the greatest number of England vs Australia Test matches.

4. For which English county did Ted McDonald, the Australian fast bowler of the 1920–21 series, play?

SIXES

1. Which player was dismissed first ball in his only Test innings in an Ashes Test match?

2. Name the player who played one Test match for England in 1921, and collapsed and died at the wicket whilst batting in a wartime match at Lord's.

See Answers on pages 134–5.

1924–1926

SINGLES

1. Which series saw the eight-ball over introduced in Australia?

2. Who was the first batsman to bat though an entire day's play in an Ashes Test match?

3. Name the first batsman to score four hundreds in a five-Test match Ashes rubber.

4. Who was the first wicket-keeper to make four stumpings in a Test match?

5. What is the greatest number of runs scored in an over by an Australian batsman in an Ashes series?

a) 21   b) 23   c) 25

6. In 1924–5, which bowler took the most wickets by an England bowler in a series in Australia up to this time?

7. Which two Australians put on 127 for the tenth wicket at Sydney in the first Test match of 1924–5 at Sydney, a record against all countries by Australia?

8. In which year did Jack Hobbs score his only Test 100 at The Oval against Australia?

9. Name the Australian who scored a century before lunch at Headingly in 1926.

10. Who was the first batsman to score 2,000 runs against Australia?

11. Which England captain of the 1924–5 tour later became a much-loved commentator?

12. Who was the first batsman to score a hundred in each innings of a Test match against Australia?

13. Who was the first wicket-keeper to take four stumpings in a Test match?

14. Who was the captain of England in 1926 when the team won back the Ashes from Australia?

15. Which celebrated cricketer was recalled for the decisive Test match of the 1926 Ashes series at the age of 48?

16. At The Oval in 1926, which player completed a run of 52 unbroken Test appearances for England since 1909?

17. Who was the first batsman to score three centuries in a Test series in England?

18. In taking over the England captaincy from A.W. Carr at Old Trafford in the fourth Test match of 1926, who became the first professional to lead England since Arthur Shrewsbury in 1886–7?

19. In 1926, who beat the record aggregate of 2,660 runs in Tests between England and Australia, previously held by Clem Hill?

20. Which England pair shared 11 century-opening partnerships against Australia?

FOURS

1. Where and when was an Ashes Test rained off after just 50 minutes of play?

2. Which Australian leg-spinner, who went on to become the first player to take 200 Test wickets, made his debut in the 1924–5 series?

3. Who is the oldest player to score a hundred for Australia vs England?

4. How tall was Harold Larwood?

a) 6 ft 3 in.   b) 5 ft 10 in.   c) 5ft 7½ in.

SIXES

1. What is the record aggregate by a visiting England batsman in a series in Australia?

2. Who was the first batsman to score four hundreds in five Test match Ashes rubbers?

See Answers on pages 135–6.

1928–1929

SINGLES

1. What was the first-ever match to be played over eight days, and was the longest match played in Australia (33 hours, 17 minutes)?

2. Who is the oldest batsman to score a century in Ashes Test cricket?

3. What is the highest aggregate by an England batsman in an Ashes series?

4. Who is the youngest player to score a century in Tests between England and Australia?

5. Who was the oldest Australian to make his Test debut at Sydney in 1928–9?

6. In the first Test match of the 1928–9 Ashes series, which wicket-keeper set a World Test record by not conceding a bye whilst 863 runs were scored?

7. Which two batsmen hold the record for the fastest Australian 50 vs England?

8. Who replaced Don Bradman when he was dropped following his debut Test match at Brisbane in 1928–9?

9. On the 1928–9 tour, which player described Don Bradman as his 'bunny', having had early success against him?

10. Which two players hold the English third-wicket record against Australia?

11. Which two English batsmen put on 124 for the eighth wicket at Brisbane, in the first Test match of the 1928–9 series?

12. Which player, nicknamed 'Farmer', who bowled a slow left-arm, took 13–256 from 124.5 overs in the fourth Test of the 1928–9 series at Adelaide?

13. When was the first and only Test match on Brisbane's Exhibition Ground?

14. Which Hampshire batsman played for England on both the 1911–12 and 1928–9 tours of Australia?

15. What is the largest victory in terms of runs in an Ashes Test match?

16. Who returned his best bowling figures in an Ashes Test match in Brisbane in the first Test of the 1928–9 series?

17. Who carried his bat making 30 not out of a total of 66 for Australia at Brisbane in the first Test match of 1928–9?

18. Which England batsman has participated in the greatest number of century partnerships for England vs Australia?

19. Who is the oldest batsman to score a century in Test cricket?

20. Which former Australian cricketer was the grandfather of Ian, Greg and Trevor Chappell?

FOURS

1. Which player holds the record for the greatest number of runs scored from one ball?

2. Which Australian player with the nickname 'Dainty' held the catch that dismissed Harold Larwood for 98 when nightwatchman in 1928–9 series, in spite of his reputation as a terrible fielder?

3. Which player made five tours of Australia between 1907–8 and 1928–9 scoring 2,493 runs on these tours?

4. Which batsmen scored a century in each innings of the fourth Test at Adelaide in the 1928–9 series?

SIXES

1. In the 1928–9 series at Melbourne, who scored a hundred in his first Test match against Australia and later scored a century in his last match against them in 1938?

2. Which player in the 1928–9 series scored 779 runs in 5 innings?

See Answers on pages 136–7.

7 The Golden Age: 1896–1914

Probably the best series in Australia, in the first 30 years of Test cricket, was that captained by the all-round sportsman, Andrew Stoddart, whose team of talented players narrowly took the 1894–5 series, 3–2. It was this tour that fully ushered in The Golden Age of Cricket, which is deemed officially to have started in 1895.

Although uncovered wickets were the norm, cricket was played with considerable panache and offered great variety. With the end of W.G. Grace's Test career before the turn of the century, the baton was handed not to an Englishman, but to Victor Trumper, one of the most dynamic batsmen of this or any age. His consummate ability on drying wickets was truly inspirational, and he was unrelenting in his attack as a batsman, notching up six Ashes centuries.

Trumper was by no means alone in bringing about Australia's new-found success. Cricket in Australia had benefited greatly from the emergence of the Sheffield Shield competition in the early 1890s and the establishment of regular match-play between states. As well as Trumper, Australia could boast several more great players including Warren Bradley, Clem Hill – the first great Australian left-hander – Warwick Armstrong, Syd Gregory, Monty Noble and Reggie Duff, backed up by strong bowling from the likes of Hugh Trumble, Frank Laver, Jack Saunders, 'Tibby' Cotter and Albert Trott.

England also had many memorable players including Kumar Shri Ranjitsinhji, Archie MacLaren, Tom Hayward and Stanley Jackson, and bowlers such as Tom Richardson, Jack Hearne, Wilfred Rhodes, Sydney Barnes, George Hirst and Colin Blythe.

With its swashbuckling style, carefree attitude and considerable displays of skill, The Golden Age is considered by many to be the high point in the history of cricket. It ended with the First World War, after which the game was never quite the same.

1896–1901

SINGLES

1. When and where did five England players threaten strike action in a dispute over match fees for a match Test against Australia?

2. Who was the first Indian-born cricketer to play in a Test match for England?

3. In 1897–8, who became the first player to score 500 runs in an Ashes series?

4. Which England player, in the 1897–8 series against Australia, kept wicket and also bowled slow leg-breaks in four Tests?

5. Name the England captain who went on the 1894–5 and 1897–8 tours of Australia and later committed suicide at the age of 52?

6. Which England player known as 'The Surrey Catapult' took 8 for 94 on his last appearance in a Test match at Sydney in 1897–8?

7. Who, in his 15 Test matches against Australia, scored 989 runs at an average of 44.95 – one of the highest averages in the first 25 years of Test cricket?

8. Which player, who later became the oldest-ever England Test cricketer, made his debut in W.G. Grace's last Test match in 1899 at Nottingham?

9. In 1897–8, who was the first player called for throwing in an Ashes Test match?

10. Clem Hill holds the record for the highest score made by a batsman under 21 in England vs Australia Test matches, scoring 188 at Melbourne in the fourth Test of 1897–8. How old was he?

a) 17   b) 18   c) 20

11. In 1897–8, Joe Darling scored the fastest century for Australia vs England. How long did he take?

a) 91 minutes
b) 101 minutes
c) 121 minutes

12. Who was the first player in an Ashes Test match to reach his century with a six (and hitting the ball right out of the ground)?

13. Which player recorded the first Ashes century of the 20th century?

14. Which Australian player made the only century during Sheffield's one and only Test match at the Bramall Lane ground?

15. Which player captained the England team of 1902 – regarded as the strongest batting side ever to take the field against Australia – with all 11 players having scored centuries in first-class cricket?

16. Who was the first wicket-keeper to claim eight dismissals in a Test match?

17. Which Test match was abandoned for the day following a dust storm?

18. What is the best match analysis achieved by an Australian in his home country?

19. What is the lowest innings score made in an England vs Australia Test match?

20. Which Australian fast bowler achieved his best Test performance at Lord's in 1899 with figures of 7–88?

FOURS

1. Before Don Bradman, which batsman had scored the highest number of runs on the opening day of an England vs Australia Test match?

2. Which two English batsmen were involved in the last-wicket partnership at The Oval in 1902 match against Australia when the famous quote 'We'll get them in singles' is alleged to have been made, before England won by one wicket?

3. Which unknown bowler, plucked from obscurity, took 5–65 on his debut for Archie MacLaren's side at Sydney in the first Test match of 1901–2?

4. Which Test bowler took 13–244 in the Old Trafford Test in 1896 – his best-ever Test match figures?

SIXES

1. In the first Test at Sydney of the 1897–98 series, who are the two Australians who still hold the record for the ninth wicket in both Ashes Tests and for Australia in all Test matches?

2. When did the last privately-organized England team play Tests in Australia and who was the captain?

See Answers on pages 138–9.

1902–1908

SINGLES

1. Which Australian bowler took his second Test-match hat-trick in his last first-class match?

2. Which was the first touring team to be selected and managed by the MCC?

3. Which player, on his debut, achieved the then-highest score both for England vs Australia and for any Test match?

4. What is the record tenth-wicket partnership in Ashes cricket?

5. What is the best match analysis for England in Australia?

6. What is the highest aggregate total of runs on debut by a player in England vs Australia matches?

7. Which player was described as a 'genius without compare; the finest and most-loved player of his time, whose modesty and generosity off the field was just as praiseworthy'? And who said it?

8. Which England captain, later to be Governor of Bengal, topped both the batting and bowling averages in the 1905 series against Australia?

9. Which England wicket-keeper, who played in 25 Ashes Test matches, had 61 victims including 18 stumpings?

10. Which two opposing captains were born on the same day?

11. Who was the last player in an Ashes Test match to take a wicket with his first ball in Test cricket?

12. What is the greatest aggregate of runs by an Australian in an England vs Australia Test series prior to the First World War?

13. Which celebrated batsman, who once held the record for the world's highest individual score in Test cricket, also played international football for England and captained them at both sports?

14. Which Australian captain was named the Wisden Cricketer Of The Year in 1908?

15. Which player has scored the most runs by a number 9 batsman in Ashes Tests?

16. What is the fastest century in England vs Australia Test matches and who scored it?

17. Which bowler bowled unchanged in both innings of an Ashes Test match?

18. Who was the first Australian to score four Test match centuries against England?

19. Which bowler invented the googly, and was largely responsible for England winning two of its first three Test matches?

20. Who was Victor Trumper's opening partner in the fastest-ever century-opening partnership of 57 minutes at Old Trafford in 1902?

FOURS

1. Which two batsmen hold the Australian eighth-wicket record of 243 against all Test-playing countries, for their partnership in the third Test of the 1907–8 tour at Adelaide?

2. Who was the first Australian to score 50 and take 10 wickets in an Ashes Test?

3. In 1902, who scored the first century before lunch in an Ashes Test match?

4. In the Test of 1902 at Old Trafford, which player – who went on to father a celebrated England player – dropped an important catch, and was then bowled with only four runs needed for England to beat Australia, resulting in an Australian victory by three runs?

SIXES

1. In which Ashes Test match did England's last pair add 39, winning the match by one wicket, and who were the batsmen?

2. Which player, not in the original MCC England Touring Team, was called up and achieved top scores in both innings, as well as scoring a century on debut?

See Answers on pages 139–40.

1909–1914

SINGLES

1. When was the first timeless Test match played in England?

2. Which England player scored the first 100 by a left-hander against Australia?

3. What is the highest opening partnership for England in England vs Australia matches?

4. Which England bowler took 5 wickets for 6 runs in 11 overs, having dismissed Warren Bardsley with the first ball of the match?

5. Which captain emulated F.S. Stanley Jackson's feat in winning all five tosses in the 1909 Ashes series?

6. Who was appointed Selection Chairman for the Australian Board of Control and promptly appointed himself vice-captain of the 1909 tour of England?

7. Name the six Australian players who, in 1912, went on strike in protest at the Board of Control's decision not to reappoint Frank Laver as manager of the 1912 tour?

8. Which celebrated all-round sportsman and Golden-Age hero captained England in the 1912 Triangular Series against Australia and South Africa?

9. What is the highest aggregate made by a batsman in a series of Ashes Tests prior to the First World War, and by whom?

10. In 1915, which much-loved Australian player died of Bright's disease at the age of 37?

11. Which two players hold the English seventh-wicket record against Australia?

12. Which leg-spinning dentist, who made his debut for Australia at the age of 28, took 12 wickets on his debut, and 32 in the 1911–12 series?

13. Name the two England bowlers who took 34 and 32 wickets respectively in the 1911–12 series that England won 4–1.

14. What is the best individual bowling analysis by an Australian in England?

15. Who took 77 of his 106 Ashes wickets on three tours of Australia in 1901–2, 1907–8 and 1911–12?

16. Who captained England on the tours to Australia in 1903–4 and 1911–12, and was the manager of the 1932–3 tour?

17. Who was the first batsman to score a century in each innings of an Ashes Test?

18. Name the England player who, aged 37 and in his first season in county cricket as a googly-bowler, took 3–19 in his first 7 overs of his only Test, ending with 5–146 and 2–136?

19. Whose best match-figures in Test cricket were taken in the deciding match of the 1912 Triangular tournament at The Oval in the third Test against Australia?

20. After scoring 136 in the fifth Test match of 1909 at The Oval, who waited 17 years before scoring his next century against England?

FOURS

1. Which pre-First World War bowler took 106 wickets in 20 Ashes Tests at an average of 21.58 with 12 five-wicket innings and one ten-wicket match?

2. Which two English left-arm bowlers dismissed all 20 Australians between them in the first Test match at Edgbaston in 1909?

3. Which player in the second Test at Melbourne in the 1911–12 series is the second-youngest player to score a century for England against Australia?

4. Who was recalled, at the age of 41, to lead the 1912 Australia team following the withdrawal of the six rebels?

SIXES

1. By the start of the First World War, how many tests had been played in the England vs Australia series, and what were the total number of wins and losses of each side?

2. Which two bowlers took 66 wickets between them to help win the 1911–12 series for England, 4–1?

See Answers on pages 140–41.

8 The Early Years: Pre-1896

The first match between Australia and England – deemed to have been the very start of Test cricket – took place in March 1876 in Melbourne. This began the series that ultimately became the fight for the Ashes, and was played between an England team captained by the Sussex all-rounder James Lillywhite, and an Australian combined team consisting of players from Victoria and New South Wales. Lillywhite's team had been the first to play eleven-a-side matches in Australia, and mid-tour travelled to New Zealand, where they played a further eight matches.

There was considerable controversy as to the make-up of the Australian team, with local rivalries being stirred by the fact that the sole selector, Jack Conway, was from Victoria (incidentally, he had played against one of the earlier England touring teams led by H.H. Stephenson in the 1861–2 series). Until 1876, all matches had been played against odds, and the ultimate selection deprived the first Australian team of Billy Murdoch, Fred Spofforth and Ted Evans, all of whom had played for the successful Fifteen of the NSW side that had beaten Lillywhite's team earlier on the tour. With the withdrawal of the outstanding fast bowler Frank Allan, the friction of interstate rivalry between the teams and, subsequently states, had been spawned and was to continue for many years.

1876–1880

SINGLES

1. Name the player who bowled the first ball in Test cricket.

2. During the first Test match at Melbourne in the 1876–7 series, who faced the first ball and scored the first run (second ball)?

3. Who was the oldest player to make his Test debut in an England vs Australia match in 1876–7?

4. The same match also featured the youngest-ever player to appear in an England vs Australia Test match. How old was he?

5. Name the American-born player in the first-ever England vs Australia Test match at Melbourne in 1876–7?

6. What was the similarity between the first-ever England vs Australia Test match and the Centenary Test match at Melbourne in 1977?

7. In the first-ever Test match between England and Australia in 1876–7, which player should have kept wicket but was arrested following a fight over a bet in New Zealand, and was awaiting trial when the Test match began?

8. Which opening batsman played as wicket-keeper in the first-ever Test match, replacing the original selected England wicket-keeper?

9. Who captained England in the first-ever Test match at Melbourne in 1876–7?

10. Name his opposing captain.

11. Where was the first England vs Australia Test match played in England?

12. Who became the first player to score two fifties in a Test match?

13. Which player scored the first-ever century in England vs Australia matches?

14. Who achieved the first Test hat-trick in the third Test match to be played?

15. In 1880, on his debut against Australia at The Oval, who scored England's first Test-match century?

16. When was the first instance of three brothers playing in the same Test match?

17. Who became the first Test captain to score a hundred in his first match as captain?

18. Name the first player to retire due to an injury in Test cricket.

19. Who was England's leading scorer in the first three Test matches played?

20. Who captained England in the third-ever Test match in 1878–9?

FOURS

1. Who was the first substitute in Test cricket?

2. Which Secretary of Surrey was responsible for organizing the first-ever Test match in England in 1880, negotiating the staging with Lord Harris and Billy Murdoch?

3. Who shared the first century partnership in Test cricket?

4. Who was the first Test-match umpire subsequently to play Test cricket?

SIXES

1. Which player, appearing in one Test match for England vs Australia at Melbourne in 1879, was killed 20 years later by a misplaced load of sugar as it was being transported onto a ship at Port of Spain, Trinidad?

2. What is the highest individual proportion of any Test innings in terms of total team runs scored?

See Answers on pages 141–2.

1881–1889

SINGLES

1. Who was the first bowler to take 14 wickets in a Test match?

2. At Sydney in 1886–7, England scored their lowest Test score in an Ashes series. What was it?

a) 35   b) 45   c) 55

3. Who was the first batsman to top score in both innings of a Test match?

4. Which England captain's girlfriend initiated the Ashes on the 1882–3 tour of Australia, with the first fight for the Ashes being in England in 1884?

5. Who was the first number 11 batsman to score a 50 in both Test cricket and Australian first-class cricket?

6. Who played in all of the first 17 Test matches between Australia and England?

7. The first Test match was played at Adelaide in which year?

8. Who scored the first double century in Test cricket?

9. Which batsman achieved the highest score ever made by a number 10 batsman in Ashes Test cricket?

10. In which Test match did all 11 players bowl for England?

11. In what year was the first Test match played at Lord's?

12. Who was the first wicket-keeper to score two 50s in a Test match?

13. Name the player who achieved the first Test hat-trick by an England bowler?

14. Who was the first player to score a 50 and take ten or more wickets in a Test match?

15. Which match caused the Ashes to come into being and why?

16. When was the first instance of two bowlers bowling unchanged in a completed Test innings?

17. Which players participated in the first century-opening partnership in Test cricket?

18. The first England vs Australia match of 1884 was held at which ground?

19. Name the first former Test cricketer to umpire a Test match.

20. Who was the first bowler to take eight wickets in an innings in an Ashes Test match?

FOURS

1. Which England player refused to bowl in the third Test match of the 1884–5 series at Sydney, on a pitch ideally suited to him, because of a quarrel with his captain Arthur Shrewsbury?

2. Which player scored the first century at Adelaide in the first Test match played there in 1884–5?

3. At The Oval in 1884, which England wicket-keeper took off his pads, and whilst bowling lobs took 4–19, which proved to be his only first-class wickets?

4. Following the 1888 tour of England, who were the first two Australians to be made Wisden Cricketers of the Year in the 1889 *Almanack*?

SIXES

1. Who was the first Tasmanian to play Test cricket for Australia?

2. When and where was the shortest completed Test match in Ashes history, taking only 6 hours and 34 minutes of playing time?

See Answers on pages 143–4.

1890–1895

SINGLES

1. Name the first England batsman to carry his bat through a Test innings.

2. In making 67 runs in a completed day's Test cricket and ultimately batting 448 minutes for 91, who achieved the slowest completed innings in all first-class cricket?

3. In which series did Australia win the Ashes for the first time?

4. Name the series in which the six-ball over was introduced in Australia for Test cricket?

5. Which batsman scored the fastest-ever half-century in Test cricket?

6. Which was the first Test match in which no byes were conceded?

7. In the 1894–5 series, which Australian all-rounder scored 475 runs and took 34 wickets?

8. Which player made a hundred on his Test debut at Lord's in 1893 for Australia, and also scored a century on his home debut against England at Sydney in the fourth Test of 1894–5?

9. When was the first Test match to be watched by more than 100,000 spectators?

10. Which English team touring Australia and captained by W.G. Grace was known as Lord Sheffield's team?

11. Which player made the first declaration in Test cricket?

12. In the 1894–5 series, which Test match had to be delayed because a number of England players had drunk too much the night before?

13. Name the first Australian to make a Test century at Lord's.

14. Which Australian player was the first to take 100 wickets in Test matches versus England?

15. Who was known as Australia's W.G. Grace?

16. When was the first occurrence of a Test match in an Ashes series being won after a side had followed on?

17. Who scored the first double century in a Test match in Australia?

18. During the 1880s and 1890s, which Australian made five tours to England?

19. In the 1893 Lord's Test match, who became the first umpire to officiate in Tests in more than one country?

20. Which outstanding all-round sportsman, who was both a rugby international and Test cricketer, captained England to victory in the 1894–5 series, and at the time held the record for the highest score made in club cricket?

FOURS

1. Who was the first Australian batsman to carry his bat through a Test innings?

2. Which Lancastrian made six tours of Australia in the 1880s and 1890s for England?

3. Name the player who achieved the best bowling analysis on debut in an Ashes Test match?

4. Which Australian bowler took a wicket with his first ball in Test cricket in what was to be his only Test match?

SIXES

1. Which bowler was the first to take 12 wickets in an Ashes Test match on debut for England?

2. Name the Tasmanian selected as second wicket-keeper for the Australian tour of England in 1890, and who, it was later discovered, had never kept wicket in his life.

See Answers on pages 144–5.

9　General Knowledge

Miscellaneous 1

SINGLES

1. Who has scored the greatest number of hundreds in the Ashes series of Test matches?

2. Who is the only player to score more than one double century for England, in England vs Australia Test matches?

3. Which player has bowled the greatest number of balls in England vs Australia Test matches?

4. Which batsman reached 1,000 runs in Test cricket in the fewest number of matches, all of which were Ashes Test matches?

5. When was the first time that a country won a five-match series, having lost the first two matches?

6. What is the highest individual innings in England vs Australia Test matches?

7. Only two players have scored a 100 and taken 5 wickets in an innings in Ashes Tests. Name one of them.

8. When were the only two 5–0 whitewashes in Ashes Test matches?

9. Which Australian bowler, in his three Lord's Test matches in 1997, 2001 and 2005, took 26 wickets for 299 runs at an average of 11.50 runs per wicket?

10. Which England cricketer was vice-captain on four of his six tours to Australia, but never achieved his ambition of leading England in Australia?

11. Which player has scored the greatest number of runs and the greatest number of centuries for England vs Australia?

12. Which player achieved the fastest double of 1,000 runs and 100 wickets in England vs Australia Tests?

13. Name the batsman who had the following sequence of scores in Test matches at Sydney Cricket Ground against Australia: 251, 112, 101, 75 not out, 231 not out, 1 and 37.

14. As a result of their exploits in the Ashes series of 1956, 1975, 1981 and 2005, four cricketers have been voted BBC Sports Personality of the Year. Name two of them.

15. Who was the first batsman to score hundreds against Australia, in both his first and last Test matches against them?

a) Maurice Leyland
b) Eddie Paynter
c) Philip Mead

16. Which is the only county to have six representatives in an England team against Australia?

17. Since the Second World War, only three England captains have won an Ashes series in Australia. Name one of them.

18. What is the third-best analysis by an English bowler in an innings after Jim Laker's 10–53 and 9–37 in an Ashes Test match?

19. Which journalist placed the obituary notice in the *Sporting Times* on 2 September 1882, following the loss of the 1882 Oval Test match by England?

20. Name the wicket-keeper who has played the greatest number of Ashes Tests.

FOURS

1. How many of the 321 Test matches between England and Australia have been abandoned without a ball being bowled?

2. Who are the only two specialist wicket-keepers in the past 50 years to captain Australia in an Ashes Test match?

3. Which bowler has conceded the most runs in a Test-match innings, not only in Ashes Test matches but in the whole history of Test cricket?

4. Who was regarded as the greatest Australian batsman of the 19th century, and who was his English coach?

SIXES

1. Which England opening partners shared 11 first-wicket century-partnerships against Australia in Ashes Tests?

2. What is the lowest-fourth innings target to be successfully defended?

See Answers on pages 145–7.

Miscellaneous 2

SINGLES

1. Which Test ground used for Ashes Test matches has the highest capacity?

2. Who are the only two England captains to regain and successfully defend the Ashes?

3. Only five batsmen have scored more than 3,000 runs in England vs Australia Test matches. Name three of them.

4. Who are the only three bowlers to take more than 150 wickets in England v Australia Test matches?

5. Who was the first former Australian Test cricketer to umpire an Ashes Test match?

6. Which two England captains had the most matches without defeat against Australia?

7. What is the lowest total ever made by Australia in a Test match?

8. What is the longest period, in terms of matches, in which England have failed to beat Australia?

9. Which two pairs of brothers each scored centuries in Oval Test matches for Australia in 1972 and 2001 respectively?

10. Who is the only Englishman to take 10 wickets in a match four times against Australia?

11. Which Australian batsman was dismissed five times in the 'nervous '90s' in Tests against England?

12. Which bowler ended his two-match Test career against Australia as the most expensive wicket-taker in Test cricket, with 1–281?

13. Who are the only three opening pairs of English batsmen to share century partnerships in both innings of a Test against Australia?

14. Name the England player who appeared in the same Ashes Test match both as a player and an umpire.

15. Which Australian batsman has scored the second-highest number of centuries against England after Don Bradman?

16. Where was the closest-ever finish in terms of runs and when did it happen?

17. Who was the first batsman in Test history to hit centuries in each of two consecutive Test innings?

18. Two players have scored five hundreds against Australia in England. Name one of them.

19. Who was the first player to score 500 runs in an Ashes series without scoring a century?

20. Who was the first wicket-keeper to achieve 100 dismissals in England vs Australia Test matches?

FOURS

1. Who are the only two cricketers in England vs Australia Test matches to score centuries in each of their first two Tests?

2. Which abandoned Ashes Test match led to the first One-Day International (ODI) being played, and where did it take place?

3. Who are the two batsmen to have made a century in an England vs Australia series out of the lowest total to contain a century?

4. Which England batsman played 57 Test innings against Australia without registering a duck?

SIXES

1. In the final Test match at The Oval in 2009, apart from Jonathan Trott, three other England batsmen in the team had also made centuries on their Test debuts. Who were they?

2. Which Australian wicket-keeper cost Australia the 1985 series, when he smashed a square cut into Allan Lamb's boot, allowing David Gower to catch him out?

See Answers on pages 147–8.

Miscellaneous 3

SINGLES

1. When did the first England-team tour Australia without a Yorkshire or Lancashire county player?

2. Three Australian bowlers have taken ten wickets four times against England. Name two of them.

3. Which wicket-keeper has taken the greatest number of stumpings in England vs Australia Test matches?

4. Which player captained England on 32 occasions but never in Australia, in spite of making five tours there?

5. Which Australian player holds the record for being the captain of the team the most number of times in matches against England?

6. Name the Australian who was the first to score 1,000 runs in Test cricket, all against England?

7. Which Australian wicket-keeper later became an England Test selector?

8. When was the first five-match Test rubber in England?

9. Name the England player who made six successive tours of Australia between 1954–5 and 1974–5?

10. On which English ground is the Radcliffe Road end to be found?

11. Who was the first English captain to win all five tosses in a five-match rubber?

12. Who is the only wicket-keeper to have made more than 25 dismissals in three separate Ashes series?

13. Who are the only two Australian bowlers to have taken ten wickets in an Ashes Test match, four times?

14. Name the England player who holds the record for the most dismissals as a wicket-keeper in Test cricket?

15. Which Australian batsman scored a century on his debut against England, and also a century in his last Test innings against England?

16. Which player is the only one to have scored 200 runs and taken eight wickets in a match?

17. Who is the only English cricketer to go in first and last in an England vs Australia Test match?

18. Name the Australian and English Men of the Series in the 2005 Ashes.

19. Two players in England vs Australian Tests matches have been dismissed in the 90s in both innings. Name one of them.

20. Where was the England wicket-keeper in the 2005 Ashes winning team born, and who was he?

FOURS

1. Who are the only two bowlers to take 14 or more wickets in an Ashes Test match for Australia?

2. Five Australian batsmen have carried their bat through a completed innings against England. Name two of them.

3. Which player has the highest strike-rate and the lowest average for a bowler, having taken more than 100 wickets in Test cricket?

4. Which two Kent players on the 1974–5 tour of Australia took 11 wickets and scored a hundred respectively in the third Test match at Adelaide?

SIXES

1. Which Australian, who played two Tests in the 1936–7 series, was omitted from the 1938 tour of England and was killed in the Second World War, aged 26?

2. Having played only six first-class matches, which player was selected for the fifth Test match of the 1986–7 series and took eight wickets, scored 53 runs and won the Man of the Match Award?

See Answers on pages 148–9.

10 Trivia

Nicknames

SINGLES

1. Which celebrated Australian fast bowler was nicknamed 'Pigeon'?

2. Name the England cricketer who was nicknamed 'Beefy'.

3. One Australian player was nicknamed 'Phanto' due to his fondness for the comic book character 'The Phantom'. Who was he?

4. Which Australian captain was nicknamed 'The Big Ship'?

5. 'Nugget' was the nickname of which celebrated Australian all-rounder?

6. Which England fast bowler was also known as 'Dazzler'?

7. Which 19th-century England captain was nicknamed 'Monkey'?

8. 'Punter' was which Australian player?

9. Who, on the Australian team, was better known as 'Colonial Hercules'?

10. Which Australian opening batsman was nicknamed 'Alfie'?

11. Jack Gregory, the Australian Test cricketer, was also known as what?

12. Which cricketer was often referred to as the 'Eighth Wonder of the World'?

13. Which Australian opening batsman was called 'William the Conqueror' on the 1961 tour of England, and in 1962–3, 'The Corpse with Pads On'?

14. 'Kipper' was which England cricketer's nickname?

15. What was Steve Waugh dubbed?

16. Which South African-born England player was known as 'The Judge'?

17. Who, on the Australian team, was also known as 'Pistol'?

18. Which left-handed England opener was nicknamed 'Banger' because of his love of sausages?

19. 'Tubs' or 'Tubby' was the name given to which Australian captain?

20. Which Australian player was nicknamed 'Dizzy'?

FOURS

1. Which bowler, who took 7–27 at Melbourne in 1954–5, was nicknamed 'Typhoon'?

2. One English captain added 'Dylan' to his name by deed poll, as a tribute to his favourite singer. Who was he?

3. 'Johnny Won't Hit Today' was whose nickname?

4. Which England player was known as 'The Little Governor (Guvnor)'?

SIXES

1. Which Australian batsman of the inter-war years was nicknamed 'The Rock'?

2. In the 19th century, which Australian was known as 'The Prince of Wicket-keepers'?

See Answers on pages 149–50.

Books and the Media

SINGLES

1. Whose autobiography was called *Under the Southern Cross*?

2. Which Australian captain wrote a series of diaries chronicling his years at the crease?

3. After 42 years as a commentator, which ex-Australian captain completed his last commentary in Britain during the final Test of the Ashes series of 2005?

4. Whose autobiography was subtitled *Don't Tell Kath*?

5. In which year did the celebrated broadcaster Brian Johnston commentate on his final Test match?

6. Which England wicket-keeper has one of his paintings hanging in the Imperial War Museum in London?

7. Name the former Australian Test cricketer who wrote the book *Brightly Fades the Don*, a tribute to Don Bradman?

8. Which celebrated England off-spinner entitled his ghosted autobiography *Over to Me*?

9. What was the name of Marcus Trescothick's award-winning autobiography of 2008?

10. In 1996, which charismatic England cricketer wrote a novel called *Deep Cover*?

11. Which former Prime Minister wrote the award-winning book, *More Than a Game: The Story of Cricket's Early Years*?

12. Which Australian fast bowler's autobiography was entitled *Menace*?

13. Name the England captain who wrote *The Art of Captaincy*.

14. Which Australian bowler recorded a duet with Indian singer Asha Bhosle, called *You're the One for Me*?

15. Which England batsman's autobiography was entitled *Rising from The Ashes*?

16. In 2009, Duncan Hamilton wrote the award-winning biography of which England cricketer of the 1930s?

17. In 2006, which superstar of the game made an appearance in *Neighbours*?

18. In which year did the BBC first broadcast ball-by-ball commentary of a Test match?

19. Which former England captain's autobiography was called *Playing with Fire*?

20. Whose final book was called *The Art of Cricket*?

FOURS

1. Which celebrated commentator completed his 35-year career on the 1980 Centenary Test at Lord's?

2. The Ashes urn features in which science-fiction comedy novel by Douglas Adams?

3. Which cricketer appeared in an episode of the TV sitcom *Dad's Army*?

4. Who wrote *In Quest of the Ashes*?

SIXES

1. Whose autobiography was entitled *Out of My Comfort Zone*?

2. The Ashes feature in a 1953 film based on a play by Terence Rattigan. What is it called?

See Answers on pages 150–1.

Pot Luck

SINGLES

1. What is Don Bradman's middle name?

2. Who is recognized as the first streaker in an Ashes Test match?

3. In 1937, who was the first cricketer to be knighted?

4. Who is the only Australian cricketer ever to be knighted?

5. Which Australian Test ground is nicknamed 'The Gabba'?

6. Who is the youngest England player to play in an Ashes Test match?

7. On which ground in Australia would you find the George Giffen Stand?

8. Who is the oldest player to have captained either England or Australia in an Ashes Test match?

9. In which series was the six-ball over introduced for Test cricket?

10. Where is The Donald Bradman Museum?

11. Which England captain became the Earl of Darnley?

12. On which ground would you find the Brewongle Stand?

13. Name the ground in Australia on which the greatest number of Test matches have been played.

14. When did the first Test match at Perth take place?

15. Bruce Reid was the tallest player to appear in an Ashes Test match. How tall was he?

16. Who is the tallest player to score an Ashes century?

17. In which city is Bramall Lane, where an Ashes Test match was played in 1902?

18. Where is the Ashes urn usually kept?

19. The first Test match to have more than 100,000 spectators was in which series?

20. Which ground became the 100th to be used in Test cricket, when it hosted the first Ashes Test match in 2009?

FOURS

1. What caused a number of delays in the second Test match at Melbourne in the 1924–5 series?

2. In which South American country was F.R. 'Freddie' Brown, the captain of the 1950–1 England tour to Australia, born?

3. Which celebrated Australian Test cricketer flew as a bomber pilot of Beauforts and Mosquitoes in the Second World War?

a) Ross Gregory
b) Ray Lindwall
c) Keith Miller

4. What are the two names that feature in the penultimate line of the verse pasted on the Ashes urn?

SIXES

1. Which hero of the 1934 Lord's Test match died as a result of injuries received leading The Green Howards in the invasion of Sicily, and is buried in Caserta's Military Cemetery

2. Which England opening bowler of the 1936–7 tour to Australia was killed when his plane crashed in a training flight in the Second World War?

See Answers on pages 151–2.

Answers

1 The 21st Century: 2001–2009

2001–2004

SINGLES

1. c) 49 not out
2. Mark Butcher
3. b) 315 at the fourth Test of 2001 at Headingley, Leeds
4. Mark Butcher
5. c) Simon Jones
6. Alec Stewart
7. Matthew Hayden – 197 and 103
8. a) Martin Love
9. b) Michael Vaughan – it included three centuries
10. c) Andrew Caddick
11. Justin Langer
12. b) 11
13. a) Alec Stewart
14. Adam Gilchrist of Australia – 133, 4 ct, 1 st at Sydney
15. Mark Ramprakash
16. Adam Gilchrist
17. 8
18. Justin Langer with 250
19. Shane Warne
20. Steve Waugh

FOURS

1. Launceston, Tasmania
2. Mike Atherton, when Nasser Hussain was injured

3. Chris Silverwood
4. Jimmy Ormond

SIXES

1. Usman Afzaal, in the first Test match
2. Craig White of England dismissed Darren Lehmann of Australia

2005–2007

SINGLES

1. Glenn McGrath, when dismissing Marcus Trescothick
2. Duncan Fletcher
3. Glenn McGrath
4. a) Andrew Flintoff for his 68 and 73, 7 wickets and 2 catches
5. Kevin Pietersen – 57 and 64 not out
6. Shane Warne – 90
7. England won by 2 runs
8. c) 407
9. Geraint Jones
10. Shane Warne
11. 9 – a record in an Ashes Test
12. Shane Warne, when he dismissed Marcus Trescothick
13. Matthew Hayden – 138
14. Kevin Pietersen
15. Andrew Flintoff
16. Andrew Flintoff
17. Steve Harmison
18. Andrew Flintoff was stumped by Adam Gilchrist
19. Adam Gilchrist, 102 not out in 57 balls
20. Ricky Ponting

FOURS

1. Matthew Hoggard
2. Geraint Jones
3. Monty Panesar, 5–92
4. c) Paul Collingwood

SIXES

1. Gary Pratt
2. Troy Cooley

2009

SINGLES

1. Ricky Ponting
2. Jimmy Anderson – 21 not out, and Monty Panesar – 7 not out
3. Stuart Broad, aged 23 and 25 days
4. b) 1934 – in fact it was only England's second victory at Lord's since 1896
5. Rudi Koertzen of South Africa
6. Andrew Flintoff, 5–92 in Australia's second innings
7. G.A. 'Graham' Manou (Haddin breaking a finger in practice)
8. Andrew Flintoff
9. Shane Watson, who scored 62 and 53
10. Stuart Broad
11. Michael Clarke and Andrew Strauss
12. I.J.L. 'Jonathan' Trott
13. James Anderson
14. Stuart Broad
15. Marcus North, who was also 'Man of the Match'
16. Michael Clarke – 448 for Australia, and Andrew Strauss – 474 for England
17. 8 by Australia, 2 by England
18. Due to injury – an Achilles tendon operation being required
19. Michael Clarke and Marcus North
20. Ricky Ponting, for 150 at Cardiff, in the first match of the series

FOURS

1. Paul Collingwood
2. 3–47 by Ben Hilfenhaus of Australia in England's first innings
3. Ben Hilfenhaus – 22, Peter Siddle – 20, and Mitchell Johnson – 20
4. W.L. 'Billy' Murdoch in the 19th century

SIXES

1. Simon Katich – 122, Ricky Ponting – 150, Marcus North – 125 not out, Brad Haddin – 121 not out in the first innings
2. Graham Onions, who dismissed Shane Watson and Ricky Ponting

2 Australian Supremacy: 1989–1999

1989–1991

SINGLES

1. b) David Gower
2. Allan Border
3. Steve Waugh, who scored 177 not out, 152 not out, and 21 not out before being dismissed by Angus Fraser for 43 at Edgbaston in the third Test match
4. Edgbaston in the third Test match of 1989
5. c) Devon Malcolm at Trent Bridge, 1–166
6. 1989 – Mark Taylor with 839, Dean Jones with 566, Robin Smith with 553 and Steve Waugh with 506
7. Terry Alderman – 42 for Australia in England in 1981, and 41 in England in 1989
8. Old Trafford – 1989 in the fourth Test match
9. b) 61 in Australia's innings of 602 for 6 declared at Trent Bridge in the fifth Test of 1989
10. Mark Taylor
11. a) John Stephenson
12. Steve Waugh
13. R.C. 'Jack' Russell, who scored 128 not out
14. David Gower
15. Graham Gooch – 117
16. c) 3,000
17. Adelaide
18. R.C. 'Jack' Russell (six catches)
19. Mike Atherton
20. Trevor Hohns

FOURS

1. Geoff Marsh (138) and Mark Taylor (219), who put on 329 for the first wicket for Australia at Trent Bridge, Nottingham
2. Mike Atherton (424 minutes), batting in all for 451 minutes for his 105
3. Craig McDermott
4. Mark Taylor, with 839 in six Tests in the 1989 series

SIXES

1. Geoff Marsh and Mark Taylor, who scored 301 unbroken in the first Test at Trent Bridge in 1989
2. Phil Tufnell

1993–1995

SINGLES

1. Graham Thorpe – 114 not out
2. Ian Healy at Nottingham in the first Test
3. Mark Waugh and Mike Atherton
4. Shane Warne bowled Mike Gatting at Old Trafford, Manchester
5. Alec Stewart
6. Tim May
7. Michael Slater and Mark Taylor
8. David Boon
9. Allan Border – 200 not out (fourth Test) at Headingley in 1993
10. 55, by Shane Warne 34 and Tim May 21 in the 1993 series
11. Steven Rhodes
12. Graham Gooch at Old Trafford in first Test match of 1993
13. Shane Warne, who dismissed Phil DeFreitas, Darren Gough and Devon Malcolm
14. Steve Waugh, in the first innings
15. Mike Gatting and Graham Gooch
16. David Boon – 164 at Lord's, 101 at Trent Bridge and 107 at Headingley
17. Allan Border with 200 not out, and Steve Waugh with 157 not out
18. 10

19. b) Mike Atherton – 553
20. Shane Warne

FOURS

1. Robin Smith
2. Matthew Hayden
3. Peter Such, 6–67 in the first innings
4. Graeme Hick – 98 not out; captain was Mike Atherton

SIXES

1. Andrew Caddick and Brendon Julian
2. Martin McCague and Mark Ilott

1997–1999

SINGLES

1. Nasser Hussain – 207 and Graham Thorpe – 138
2. Glenn McGrath
3. c) 77
4. Steve Waugh – 108 and 116
5. Alec Stewart at Old Trafford in the third Test match of 1997
6. Matthew Elliott
7. Adam and Ben Hollioake
8. Mike Atherton
9. Australia's Ian Healy, in the Melbourne Test of 1998–9
10. Dean Headley
11. Jason Gillespie
12. Michael Slater
13. b) Alec Stewart
14. 29
15. Alan Mullally
16. b) Ricky Ponting
17. a) Warren Hegg
18. c) Mark Taylor
19. Stuart McGill
20. Matthew Nicholson

FOURS

1. Phil Tufnell 11–93, and Andrew Caddick 8–118, at The Oval in the sixth Test of the 1997 series
2. Graham Thorpe, Mark Lathwell, Martin McCague and Mark Ilott
3. Mike Smith
4. The fourth day of the Melbourne Test match of 1998–9, taking 8 hours and 2 minutes of actual playing time. The washout on the first day allowed the ICC to extend each day's play by 1 hour 30 minutes, and Australia also claimed the extra half-hour

SIXES

1. Shaun Young
2. Dean Headley played for England, following in the footsteps of his grandfather, George Headley, and father, Ron Headley, who both played for the West Indies

3 The Packer Revolution: 1977–1988

1977–1980

SINGLES

1. a) Geoffrey Boycott – 99 not out, out of 215 at Perth in 1979–80 (first Test)
2. Derek Randall – 174
3. Rodney Hogg
4. Ian Botham and Greg Chappell
5. a) Geoffrey Boycott, 147.33 for 442 runs, five innings, two not-outs, 442 runs, 191 being his highest score
6. Tony Greig
7. Bob Willis, 7–78
8. c) 417 by England in the fourth innings of the Centenary Test at Melbourne in 1976
9. Rodney Hogg
10. Geoff Miller

11. Graham Gooch
12. Dennis Lillie in the first Test match of the 1979–80 series at Perth
13. Geoffrey Boycott in the third Test of the 1977 season at Trent Bridge, or Kim Hughes at Lord's in the 1980 Centenary Test
14. Chappell – Ian, Greg and Trevor
15. Dennis Lillee
16. b) 123 minutes
17. Geoffrey Boycott, with 191 at Headingley, Leeds
18. Chris Old
19. Ian Botham
20. Kim Hughes

FOURS

1. Derek Randall at Sydney – fourth Test of 1978–9, 406 minutes with 353 balls
2. b) 4
3. Mick Malone
4. David Hookes

SIXES

1. Tom Brooks
2. Hans Ebeling, former Australian bowler and MCC committee member

1981–1985

SINGLES

1. a) 1981 in the first Test between England and Australia at Trent Bridge, Nottingham
2. R.G.D. 'Bob' Willis
3. b) 28
4. Ian Botham
5. England vs Australia at Headingley in 1981, with England winning by 18 runs
6. No batsman scored a 50
7. Alan Knott

8. c) C.J. Tavare
9. Ian Botham – with 6 in his innings of 118 in the second innings of the fifth Test match at Old Trafford, Manchester
10. Allan Border, who took 377 minutes to reach his hundred, during an innings of 123 not out – the slowest ever by an Australian in 415 matches
11. Terry Alderman
12. Graham Dilley
13. Ian Botham in his 41st Test match
14. Dirk Wellham – 103 in the second innings
15. Terry Alderman
16. Kepler Wessels – 162 and 46 against England at Brisbane in the second Test match of 1982–3
17. Greg Chappell
18. Rodney Marsh – 28 in the 1982–3 series
19. Alan Knott, Paul Downton and Rob Taylor
20. Ian Botham

FOURS

1. Paul Parker
2. Geoff Lawson
3. Chris Tavare, who scored 89 and 9
4. David Gower – 215 in the fifth Test match

SIXES

1. Mike Whitney
2. Dennis Lillee and Rodney Marsh

1985–1988

SINGLES

1. The Oval
2. b) David Gower – 732 (average 81.33) in 1985
3. Gladstone Small
4. Chris Broad scored 162 at Perth, 116 at Adelaide and 112 at Melbourne

5. C.J. 'Jack' Richards
6. Bruce Reid of Australia who was 6 ft 8 in.
7. Ian Botham
8. Merv Hughes
9. Allan Border – 196
10. Chris Broad at Sydney in 1987–8
11. Bob Holland
12. Ian Botham scored 22 (2, 2, 4, 6, 4, 4) against Merv Hughes at Brisbane – the first Test of the 1986–7 series
13. Bob Taylor
14. c) Craig McDermott, aged 20 years and 113 days, took 8–141
15. Ian Botham
16. David Gower (215) and Tim Robinson (148), who put on 331 for the second wicket
17. Ian Botham, when he caught David Boon in the second innings
18. C.J. 'Jack' Richards
19. Mike Gatting on the 1986–7 tour, winning the series 2–1
20. David Gower

FOURS

1. Tim Robinson
2. Arnie Sidebottom
3. Bob Holland
4. Peter Taylor

SIXES

1. James Whittaker
2. Phil DeFreitas, aged 20 years, 269 days in the first Test of the 1986–7 series

4   The Post-War Years: 1950–1975

1950–1956

SINGLES

1. Lindsay Hassett
2. Jim Laker – 46 in 1956 at an average of 9.60 per wicket
3. Willie Watson and Trevor Bailey
4. Jimmy Burke
5. Tony Lock
6. Cyril Washbrook, Denis Compton and David Sheppard
7. Denis Compton
8. Stretford End
9. Lord's in the second Test match in 1956
10. 1954–5
11. Len Hutton in 1953
12. Trevor Bailey
13. Neil Harvey
14. A.S.M. 'Alan' Oakman
15. Peter Richardson of England
16. Alec Bedser, who dismissed Arthur Morris
17. F.R. 'Freddie' Brown
18. Colin Cowdrey
19. Ian Johnson
20. Willie Watson

FOURS

1. Peter Richardson – 81 and 73 at Trent Bridge, Nottingham, in 1956
2. Frank Tyson and Brian Statham
3. Jack Iverson
4. Len Hutton

SIXES

1. Jack House
2. Alec Bedser, with 39 wickets

1958–1966

SINGLES

1. a) Neil Harvey
2. a) Raman Subbe Row – 112 at Edgbaston, Birmingham, and 137 at The Oval, both in 1961
3. Peter May – 113
4. Brisbane in 1958–9
5. 106 on the fourth day at Brisbane in 1958–9, England advancing from 92–2 to 198 all out
6. c) Fred Trueman at Sydney
7. b) Peter Burge
8. a) Bob Cowper – 307 against England in 1965–6 (fifth Test)
9. Tom Veivers – 51 at Old Trafford in 1964 versus England
10. Colin Cowdrey
11. Fred Titmus and David Allen
12. Tom Vievers, with 571 balls at Manchester in 1964, and whose analysis was 95.1–36–155–3
13. Old Trafford, Manchester, in 1964: Australia 656–8 declared, England 611
14. W.M. 'Bill' Lawry in the second innings vs England at Melbourne, in the second Test match of 1962–3, taking 275 minutes to reach 50
15. R.B. 'Bobby' Simpson at Old Trafford, Manchester, in the fourth Test match of the 1964 series
16. R.W. 'Bob' Barber – 185 at Sydney on the 1965–6 tour
17. K.D. 'Doug' Walters
18. 1965–6 – Sydney (third Test) and Adelaide (fourth Test)
19. K.F. 'Ken' Barrington – this innings won the Lawrence Trophy for the fastest hundred of the Test year
20. F.S. 'Freddie' Trueman

FOURS

1. A.C. 'Archie' MacLaren – 116 at Sydney in the first Test match of 1901–2
2. Duke of Norfolk

3. Richie Benaud
4. John Edrich

SIXES

1. Neil Harvey with 167
2. Graham Corling

1968–1975

SINGLES

1. Mike Denness
2. Jim Laker – 46 in 1956 at an average of 9.60 per wicket
3. Ian and Greg Chappell
4. Fred Titmus
5. Bobby Simpson and Ken Barrington
6. David Steele
7. Bob (R.A.L.) Massie 16 – 137 (8–84 and 8–53)
8. Headingley in 1975 when campaigners for the Free George Davis campaign dug up the pitch
9. a) R.G.D. 'Bob' Willis
10. b) Keith Stackpole – 207 in 1970–71
11. Headingley in 1972
12. Graham Gooch
13. Greg Chappell – 7 at the W.A.C.A. Ground, Perth in 1974–5
14. a) Doug Walters
15. Tony Greig – 110
16. 24 by Alan Knott in 1970–71
17. Basil D'Oliveira
18. Tom Graveney
19. Ray Illingworth, as a result of John Snow being assaulted by a spectator in the seventh Test at Sydney in the 1970–71 series
20. Donald Bradman – it was his last year in the position

FOURS

1. Alan 'Froggy' Thomson and Ross Duncan

2. John Snow of England
3. Ken Eastwood
4. None

SIXES

1. Brian Luckhurst – 96 at Trent Bridge, Nottingham, in the third Test match
2. Tom Graveney for England and Barry Jarman for Australia (he was the first wicket-keeper to captain Australia since J.M. Blackham in 1894–5)

5 The Bradman Era: 1930–1948

1930–1933

SINGLES

1. 98 by Harold Larwood at Sydney, in the fifth Test of the 1932–3 series
2. 309 at Headingley, Leeds, in 1930
3. W.A. 'Bert' Oldfield
4. Eddie Paynter
5. Harry 'Bull' Alexander
6. Harold Larwood and Bill Voce
7. Bill (W.E.) Bowes
8. H. 'Dainty' Ironmonger, for Australia vs England at Sydney in 1932–3, aged 50 and 327 days on the final day of this match
9. 729–6 declared by Australia
10. W.M. 'Bill' Woodfull, scoring 155 at Lord's
11. Don Bradman – 254, 334 and 232 in the 1930 Test series
12. R.E.S. 'Bob' Wyatt
13. 214 minutes, by Don Bradman against England at Headingley, Leeds, in 1930
14. W.M. 'Bill' Woodfull – 73 not out, from a total of 193
15. In the second Test of the Bodyline series of 1932–3 at Melbourne

16. Don Bradman at Headingley in 1930
17. A.P.F. 'Percy' Chapman – 121
18. Pelham 'Plum' Warner
19. b) 139
20. Harold Larwood

FOURS

1. 451 for the second wicket by W.H. 'Bill' Ponsford – 266, and D.G. 'Don' Bradman – 244 at The Oval in 1934
2. Nawab of Pataudi Snr, who made 102
3. Lord's in 1930: Woodfull – 155, Chapman – 121
4. The *Melbourne Herald*'s High Buggy after the first day of the first Test in the 1932–3 series

SIXES

1. Sydney Copley – a member of the Nottinghamshire ground staff acting as substitute fielder for England
2. Archie Jackson, on 16 February 1933

1934–1938

SINGLES

1. An innings and 579 runs
2. Len Hutton
3. Len Hutton (364) and Maurice Leyland (187), who put on 382 for the second wicket at The Oval in 1938
4. Trent Bridge, Nottingham, in 1934, when Australia won by 238 runs
5. A.G. 'Arthur' Chipperfield at Trent Bridge, Nottingham, 1934
6. C.F. 'Cyril' Walters at Trent Bridge, Nottingham, 1934
7. Hedley Verity (7–61 and 8–43)
8. W.A. 'Bill' Brown with 512
9. b) 37 by Frank Woolley, in Australia's second innings at The Oval in 1934
10. 1896

11. W.A. 'Bill' Oldfield, who achieved it in the Lord's match of 1934
12. For the 1938 England vs Australia match at Trent Bridge, Nottingham: C.J. 'Charlie' Barnett 126; Len Hutton 100; Eddie Paynter 216 not out; and D.C.S. 'Denis' Compton, 102
13. Denis Compton, at Trent Bridge in 1938
14. J.H.W. 'Jack' Fingleton
15. W.A. Brown – 206 not out
16. c) 475 – 2 by Australia at The Oval (first day) in the fifth Test match of 1934
17. W.J. 'Bill' O'Reilly
18. Joe Hardstaff Jnr – 169 not out
19. W.R. 'Wally' Hammond
20. Don Bradman in his seventh Test match and 13 innings, all for Australia vs England

FOURS

1. C.J. 'Charlie' Barnett, who scored 98 at Trent Bridge, Nottingham, in 1938, completing his hundred off the first ball after the interval
2. Don Bradman and Bill Ponsford of Australia with 451 for the second wicket at The Oval in the fifth Test match of 1934
3. L.O. 'Chuck' Fleetwood-Smith to W.R. 'Wally' Hammond (a 'chinaman' that hit off-stump)
4. Laurie Nash, who played his one and only Test match

SIXES

1. 422 by Australia vs England at Lord's in 1938; the batsman was W.A. Bill Brown
2. Frank Woolley, recalled at the age of 47 for England vs Australia at The Oval

1946–1948

SINGLES

1. Warwickshire leg-spinner W.E. 'Eric' Hollies
2. Brisbane – Australia won by an innings and 332 runs
3. Godfrey Evans at Sydney in 1946–7

4. Don Bradman
5. J.T. 'Jack' Ikin, who took the catch at second slip off Bill Voce
6. Denis Compton – 147 and 103 not out, and Arthur Morris – 122 and 124 not out, at Adelaide in 1946–7
7. Neil Harvey – 112 at Headingley, Leeds, in the fourth Test of 1948
8. Melbourne 1946–7 (third Test)
9. Norman Yardley – 61 and 53 not out, 2–50 and 3–67, at Melbourne in 1946–7
10. N.W.D. 'Norman' Yardley
11. b) 14
12. 97 minutes
13. 404–3 to win by 7 wickets, in the fourth Test at Headingley
14. Peter Smith on the 1946–7 tour of Australia
15. Colin McCool
16. A.L. 'Lindsay' Hassett, W.A. 'Bill' Johnston, R.R. 'Ray' Lindwall, A. Morris and Don Tallon
17. 9
18. Don Bradman
19. Bill Voce
20. Alec Bedser

FOURS

1. 1932–3 at Melbourne, when he dismissed the first ball for 0 and scored 103 not out in the second innings; and, 1948 when he scored 138 and 0 at Trent Bridge, Nottingham
2. Ray Lindwall
3. Bruce Dooland
4. Donald Bradman

SIXES

1. Arthur Morris, with 696 runs, and an average of 87
2. W.J. Bill O'Reilly, who took 27

6   The Roaring Twenties: 1920–1929

1920–1923

SINGLES

1. Warwick Armstrong of Australia in 1920–21, when they had eight wins and two draws out of ten matches
2. 9–121 – taken by Arthur Mailey at Melbourne in 1920–21
3. J.W.H.T. 'Johnny' Douglas
4. Jack Gregory against England in 1920–21 with 15 catches
5. b) 30
6. Harry Makepeace for England at Melbourne in 1920–21, aged 40
7. Warwick Armstrong of Australia, who won the 1920–21 series
8. a) Frank Woolley with 95 and 93 at Lord's in 1921
9. c) Warwick Armstrong at Old Trafford, Manchester, at the fourth Test in 1921
10. Percy Holmes – 30 out of 112 at Trent Bridge, Nottingham, in 1921 (first Test)
11. Charlie Macartney
12. Warwick Armstrong at The Oval in the fifth Test of 1921 when the third day's play descended into a farce
13. J.M. 'Jack' Gregory of Australia
14. A.A. 'Arthur' Mailey with 5–160 and 5–142 at Adelaide, during the third Test of 1920–21
15. Herbie Collins
16. *The Cricketer*
17. Charlie Kelleway
18. 1,753 at Adelaide in the third Test match of 1920–21
19. Arthur Mailey, having taken 10–66 in a tour match against Gloucestershire
20. W. 'Wilfred' Rhodes, achieved in the first Test match of the 1920–21 series at Sydney

FOURS

1. Charlie Macartney

2. H.L. 'Herbie' Collins, who was 32 at the time of the first Test at Sydney in 1920–21
3. Syd Gregory
4. Lancashire

SIXES

1. Dr Roy Park for Australia vs England at Melbourne in the 1920–21 series
2. Andy Ducat

1924–1926

SINGLES

1. 1924–5, with the first actual match being the first Test at Sydney
2. Herbert Sutcliffe at Melbourne, batting through both the third and fifth days' play in the second Test of 1924–5
3. Herbert Sutcliffe, who scored 115 at Sydney (first Test), 176 and 127 at Melbourne (second Test), and 143 at Melbourne (fourth Test) during the 1924–5 series
4. W.A.S. 'Bertie' Oldfield at Melbourne in the fourth Test of the 1924–5 series
5. a) 21 by V.Y. 'Vic' Richardson off J.W.H.T. 'Johnny' Douglas at Melbourne in the second Test match of the 1924–5 series
6. Maurice (M.W.) Tate – 38
7. J.M. 'Johnny' Taylor scored 108 and A.A. 'Arthur' Mailey 46 not out
8. 1926 when he scored exactly 100 in an England victory that regained The Ashes
9. Charlie Macartney
10. J.B. 'Jack' Hobbs, in the second Test match at Melbourne in 1924–5
11. Arthur Gilligan
12. Herbert Sutcliffe – 176 and 127 at Melbourne in the second Test of the 1924–5 series
13. W.A.S. 'Bertie' Oldfield at Melbourne in the fourth Test of the 1924–5 series
14. A.P.F. 'Perry' Chapman
15. Wilfred Rhodes

16. F. E. 'Frank' Woolley
17. C.G. 'Charlie' Macartney – 133 not out at Lord's, 151 at Headingley, and 109 at Old Trafford, in the 1926 series for Australia
18. Jack Hobbs, who captained on the second and third days after Carr developed tonsillitis
19. Jack Hobbs
20. Jack Hobbs and Herbert Sutcliffe

FOURS

1. Nottingham in the first Test of 1926 with only 17.2 overs bowled
2. Clarrie Grimmett
3. Warren Bardsley with 193 not out, carrying his bat in a total of 383 at Lord's in the second Test match of 1926, aged 42 years and 202 days
4. 5 ft 7½ in.

SIXES

1. Herbert Sutcliffe with 734 runs at an average of 81.55, including four centuries, on the 1924–5 tour
2. Herbert Sutcliffe with 115 (Sydney first Test), 176 and 127 (Melbourne second Test) and 145 (Melbourne fourth Test) of the 1924–5 series

1928–1929

SINGLES

1. The fifth Test match of the 1928–9 series at Melbourne
2. Jack Hobbs when he scored 142 against Australia at Melbourne in the fifth Test match of the 1928–9 series, aged 46 years and 82 days
3. W.R. 'Wally' Hammond with 905 at an average of 113.12 in 1928–9
4. A.A. 'Archie' Jackson, who scored 164 on his Test debut aged 19 years, 152 days
5. D.D. 'Don' Blackie aged 46 years, 253 days
6. W.A.S. 'Bert' Oldfield at the Exhibition Ground, Brisbane
7. J.J. 'Jack' Lyons in the first Test of 1890 at Lord's, and Jack Ryder in the second Test match at Sydney in 1928–9, in 36 minutes

8. Otto Nothling
9. Maurice Tate
10. W.R. 'Wally' Hammond and D.R. 'Douglas' Jardine at Adelaide in the fourth Test match of 1928–9
11. E.H. 'Patsy' Hendren and Harold Larwood
12. J.C. 'Farmer' White
13. The third Test match of the 1928–9 series
14. C.P. 'Phil' Mead
15. 675 runs by England (521 and 342 – 8 declared) against Australia (122 and 66) during the first Test at Brisbane in 1928–9
16. Harold Larwood with 6–32
17. Bill Woodfull
18. Jack Hobbs
19. Jack Hobbs, when he scored 142 against Australia at Melbourne in the fifth Test match of 1928–9, aged 46 years and 82 days
20. Vic Richardson

FOURS

1. Percy Fender, with seven runs in the first Test of the 1928–9 series for England at Brisbane
2. H. 'Dainty' Ironmonger
3. Jack Hobbs
4. W.R. 'Wally' Hammond, 119 not out and 117

SIXES

1. Maurice Leyland, 137 at Melbourne
2. W.R. 'Wally' Hammond

7 The Golden Age: 1896–1914

1896–1901

SINGLES

1. In 1896 at the third Test match at The Oval. Bobby Abel, Tom Hayward and Tom Richardson relented but George Gunn and George Lohmann refused to play
2. K.S. Ranjitsinhji at Old Trafford, Manchester, in 1896
3. Joe Darling with 537 at an average of 67.13, including three centuries
4. William Storer
5. Andrew Stoddart
6. Tom Richardson
7. K.S. Ranjitsinhji between 1896 and 1902
8. Wilfred Rhodes
9. Ernie Jones of Australia in the second Test
10. c) 20
11. a) 91 minutes
12. Joe Darling at Adelaide in the third Test match of 1897–8
13. A.C. 'Archie' MacLaren who scored 116 against Australia at Sydney in December 1901
14. Clem Hill – 119 in the third Test of the 1902 series
15. A.C. 'Archie' MacLaren
16. J.J. Kelly of Australia at Sydney in the fourth Test of 1901–2
17. Australia vs England at Adelaide, the third Test of 1901–2
18. 13–77 by M.A. 'Monty' Noble, 7–17 and 6–60 at Melbourne in the second Test of the 1901–2 series
19. 36 by Australia at Birmingham in 1902 during the first Test
20. Ernie Jones

FOURS

1. Clem Hill – 182 not out at Melbourne in the fourth Test of 1897–8
2. George Hirst and Wilfred Rhodes
3. Sydney Francis Barnes
4. Tom Richardson

SIXES

1. S.E. 'Syd' Gregory and J.M. 'Jack' Blackham – 154
2. The 1901–2 team captained by Archie MacLaren

1902–1908

SINGLES

1. Hugh Trumble at Melbourne in the fifth Test match of the 1903–4 series
2. The 1903–4 team
3. R.E. 'Reginald' Foster – 287 at Sydney in the first Test of the 1903–4 tour
4. 130 – Wilfred Rhodes (40 not out) and R.E. 'Reginald' Foster (287) at Sydney in the first Test match of 1903–4
5. 15–124 by Wilfred Rhodes, 7–56 and 8–68 at Melbourne in the second Test of the 1903–4 series
6. R.E. 'Tip' Foster – 306 (287 and 19) in the first Test match at Sydney of the 1903–4 series
7. Victor Trumper, by Monty Noble
8. Stanley (F.S.) Jackson, later Sir Stanley Jackson
9. A.A. 'Arthur' Lilley
10. Hon. F.S. Jackson and Joe Darling in the 1905 series, who were both born on 21 November, 1870
11. E.J. 'Ted' Arnold, when he dismissed Victor Trumper at Sydney in 1903–4
12. 574 by Victor Trumper in the 1903–4 series
13. R.E. 'Tip' Foster, who captained England in his fifth football international and then captained England in South Africa in 1907
14. M.A. Noble
15. Clem Hill, who scored 160 at Adelaide in the third Test of 1907–8
16. G.L. 'Gilbert' Jessop (104) in 75 minutes for England at The Oval in 1902 (fifth Test match)
17. Hugh Trumble at The Oval in 1902 during the fifth Test
18. V.T. 'Victor' Trumper
19. B.J.T. 'Bernard' Bosanquet
20. R.A. 'Reginald' Duff

FOURS

1. R.J. 'Rodney' Hartigan and Clem Hill
2. Hugh Trumble – 64, 8–65 and 4–108 at The Oval in the fifth Test match of 1902
3. V.T. 'Victor' Trumper in 108 minutes in the fourth Test at Old Trafford, Manchester
4. Fred Tate (father of M.W. 'Maurice' Tate)

SIXES

1. The second Test, Melbourne, in 1907–8 – S.F. 'Sydney' Barnes and Arthur Fielder
2. George Gunn – 119 and 74 at Sydney in the first Test of 1907–8

1909–1914

SINGLES

1. The third Test of 1912, England vs Australia, at The Oval in the Triangular Tournament, which also included South Africa
2. Frank Woolley with 133 not out at Sydney in the fifth Test match of the 1911–12 series
3. 323 by J.B. 'Jack' Hobbs (178) and W. 'Wilfred' Rhodes (179) at Melbourne in the fourth Test match of the 1911–12 series (the match that regained the Ashes for England)
4. S.F. 'Sydney' Barnes at Melbourne in the second Test of 1911–12
5. Monty Noble
6. P.S. 'Percy' McAlister
7. Clem Hill, Victor Trumper, Warwick Armstrong, Vernon Ransford, H. 'Sammy' Carter and Albert 'Tibby' Cotter
8. C.B 'Charles' Fry
9. 662 at 82.75 by J.B. 'Jack' Hobbs in the 1911–12 series, including three centuries
10. Victor Trumper
11. F.E. 'Frank' Woolley and Joe Vine, with a partnership of 143 at Sydney in the fifth Test of the 1911–12 series with 143
12. H.V. 'Ranji' Hordern, 12–175 at Sydney in the first Test of 1911–12, and 32 wickets at 24 – 37 in the series

13. S.F. 'Sydney' Barnes and F.R. 'Frank' Foster
14. Frank Laver at Old Trafford, Manchester, 8–31 in the fourth Test of the 1909 series
15. Sydney Barnes
16. P.F. 'Pelham' Warner, nicknamed 'Plum'
17. Warren Bardsley, 136 and 130 at The Oval in 1909
18. D.W. Carr at The Oval in 1909 at the fifth Test match
19. Frank Woolley, 10–49 (5–29, 5–20)
20. Warren Bardsley

FOURS

1. S.F. 'Sydney' Barnes
2. G.H. 'George' Hirst and Colin Blythe with 4–28 and 5–58, and 6–44 and 5–58 respectively in the first Test match of the 1909 series at Edgbaston, Birmingham
3. J.W. 'Jack' Hearne
4. Sid Gregory

SIXES

1. 94 Tests had been played, of which Australia had won 35, and England 40, with 19 drawn
2. Sydney Barnes, who took 34 and Frank Foster who took 32

8 The Early Years: Pre-1896

1876–1880

SINGLES

1. Alfred Shaw – the Nottinghamshire round-arm length bowler
2. Charles Bannerman
3. James Southerton, who was aged 49 and 119 days when he made his debut in the first-ever match for England vs Australia at Melbourne
4. 18 years old – Tom Garrett
5. Thomas Armitage, who was born in Pullman, Chicago, USA

6. The margin of victory – 45 runs for both matches
7. E. 'Ted' Pooley
8. John Selby
9. James Lillywhite
10. D.W. 'Dave' Gregory
11. The Oval in 1880
12. George Ulyett – 52 and 63 for England vs Australia at Melbourne in 1876–77
13. Charles Bannerman – 165, at Melbourne in 1876–7 in the first-ever Test match
14. Fred Spofforth, who dismissed Vernon Royle, Francis MacKinnon and Tom Emmett in 1878–9 at Melbourne
15. W.G. Grace – 15
16. 1880 Test match at The Oval – W.G. 'William Gilbert', E.M. 'Edward Mills' and G.F. 'George Frederick' Grace
17. W.L. 'Billy' Murdoch – 153 not out at The Oval in 1880
18. Charles Bannermann 1876–7 at Melbourne
19. George Ulyett with 163 runs
20. Lord Harris

FOURS

1. William Newing for Charles Bannerman in the first-ever Test match. Newing was a professional at the Melbourne Cricket Club
2. Charles Alcock
3. W.G. Grace and A.P. Lucas – 120 for the second wicket at The Oval in 1880 for England
4. George Coulthard, who umpired the third-ever Test match at Melbourne in 1878–9 and played for Australia in the sixth-ever Test at Sydney in 1881–2 (second Test of the series)

SIXES

1. Charles Absolom
2. 67.3 per cent (69.6 per cent) of runs scored, 165 out of 245, by Charles Bannerman in the first Test match at Melbourne in 1876–7

1881–1889

SINGLES

1. F.R. Spofforth 14–90 (7–46, and 7–44) at The Oval in 1882
2. b) 45
3. Arthur Shrewsbury – 82 and 47 at Sydney in the third Test of 1881–2
4. Ivo Bligh's
5. F.R. Spofforth for Australia vs England at Melbourne in 1884–5
6. J.M. 'Jack' Blackham from 1876–7 to the first Test match of the 1884–5 tour – his run coming to a end following a dispute over gate money at Melbourne in the second Test of 1884–5
7. The first Test match of the 1884–5 series
8. W.L. 'Billy' Murdoch – 211 at The Oval in the third Test of 1884
9. W.W. Read – 117 at The Oval in 1884, reaching his hundred in 113 minutes with 36 scoring strokes
10. 1884 – third Test at The Oval
11. 1884 – the second Test match of the series
12. J.M. 'Jack' Blackham – 57 and 58 not out at Sydney in the fourth Test of 1882–3
13. William Bates, dismissing McDonnell, Giffen and Bonnor at Melbourne in the second Test match of 1882–3
14. William Barnes – 55 and 7–28 and 7–74 (14–102) at Melbourne in the second Test match of 1882–3
15. The Oval in 1882, where Australia achieved their first victory over a full-strength England side by seven runs. A mock obituary of English cricket in the *Sporting Times* concluded: 'The body will be cremated and the ashes taken to Australia.'
16. G.E. Joey Palmer (7–68) and E. Evans (3–64) for Australia vs England at Sydney in the second Test match of 1881–2
17. George Ulyett (67) and R.G. Barlow (62), who in the second innings of the second Test of the 1881–2 series at Sydney put on 122
18. Old Trafford
19. James Lillywhite, who played in the first two Test matches and first umpired in 1881–2 in the first Test match at Melbourne
20. George Lohmann 8–35 at Sydney for England vs Australia in the second Test of 1886–7

FOURS

1. A. William Flowers (England lost by 6 runs)
2. P.S. 'Percy' McDonnell
3. The Hon. Alfred Lyttelton
4. C.T.B. 'Charlie' Turner and J.J. 'Jack' Ferris

SIXES

1. Samuel Morris in the second Test match of 1884–5 at Melbourne
2. Old Trafford, Manchester, in the third Test match of 1888 with England winning by an innings and 21 runs. Eighteen wickets fell before lunch on the second day

1890–1895

SINGLES

1. Bobby Abel – 132 not out, out of 307 at Sydney in the second Test match of 1891–2
2. A.C. 'Alick' Bannerman for Australia vs England in the second Test match of 1891–2 at Sydney
3. 1891–2, winning 2 matches to 1
4. 1891–2
5. J.T. 'John Thomas' Brown, who reached 50 in 28 minutes versus Australia at Melbourne in 1894–5 in the fifth Test match of the series
6. England vs Australia, first Test at Lord's in 1890
7. George Giffen
8. H. 'Harry' Graham
9. Melbourne, for the fifth Test match of the 1894–5 series
10. The 1891–2 touring team
11. A.E. 'Andrew' Stoddart for England vs Australia at Lord's in the first Test of 1893
12. The first Test
13. Harry Graham – 107 in 1893
14. C.T.B. 'Charlie' Turner
15. George Giffen – the South Australian all-rounder

16. 1894–5 – the first Test match, when England won by 10 runs at Sydney
17. Syd Gregory – 201 at Sydney in 1894–5
18. 'Alick' Bannerman
19. James 'Jim' Phillips, who had officiated previously in Australia and was later to do so in South Africa. The next umpire to officiate in more than one country was H.D. 'Dicky' Bird in 1992–3
20. A.E. Andrew Stoddart, who scored 485 not out for Hampstead vs Stoics

FOURS

1. J. Barrett – 67 not out, out of 176 at Lord's in 1890
2. Johnny Briggs, 1896–1914
3. Albert Trott, 8–43 against England at Adelaide in 1894–5 in the third Test
4. Arthur Coningham, who dismissed A.C. 'Archie' MacLaren at Melbourne in the second Test match of 1894–5

SIXES

1. Frank Martin of Kent, 6–50, and 6–52 at The Oval in 1890
2. E.J.K. Burn, who played two Tests

9   General Knowledge

Miscellaneous 1

SINGLES

1. Donald Bradman, with a total of 19
2. W.R. 'Wally' Hammond, whose record boasts four double centuries – 251 at Sydney during the 1928–9 series, 240 at Lord's in 1938, 231 not out at Sydney during the 1936–7 series, and 200 at Melbourne during the 1928–9 series
3. Shane Warne, with 10,757 balls

4. Don Bradman – seven Test matches (thirteen innings) between 1928 and 1930
5. Australia in 1936–7 when they won 3–2
6. Len Hutton with 364 at The Oval in 1938 (fifth Test)
7. Ian Botham – 149 not out, and 6–95 at Headingley, Leeds, in 1981 (third Test); Jack Gregory – 100, and 7–69 at Melbourne in 1920–21 (second Test)
8. 1920–21 and 2006–7, with Australia the victors on both occasions
9. Glenn McGrath
10. Colin Cowdrey
11. J.B. 'Jack' Hobbs, with 3,636 runs and 12 centuries
12. Ian Botham in 22 Tests, achieved at Melbourne in 1982–3
13. W.R. 'Wally' Hammond for England
14. Jim Laker, David Steele, Ian Botham and Andrew Flintoff
15. a) Maurice Leyland – 137 at Melbourne in 1928–9, and 187 at The Oval in 1938
16. Nottinghamshire at Sydney in 1886–7 – Billy Barnes, Wilfred William Gunn, William Scotton, Mordecai Sherwin and Arthur Shrewsbury
17. Len Hutton (1954–5), Ray Illingworth (1970–71) and Mike Gatting (1986–7)
18. George Lohmann, 8–35 at Sydney in 1886–7
19. Reginald Brooks
20. Rodney Marsh – 42

FOURS

1. Three: Manchester in both 1890 and 1938, and Melbourne in 1970–71
2. Barry Jarman in 1968 and Adam Gilchrist in 2001, both at Headingley, Leeds
3. L.O.B. Fleetwood-Smith 87–11–298–1 for Australia vs England at The Oval in 1938
4. Charles Bannerman, who had been coached by William Caffyn

SIXES

1. Jack Hobbs and Herbert Sutcliffe
2. 85 by Australia at The Oval in 1882, bowling out England for 77 to achieve a 7-run victory

Miscellaneous 2

SINGLES

1. Melbourne – 100,000
2. Sir Leonard Hutton – 1953 and 1954–5. Mike Brearley – 1977 and 1978
3. Don Bradman – 5,028; Jack Hobbs – 3,636; Allan Border – 3,548; David Gower 3,269; and Steve Waugh – 3,200
4. Shane Warne – 195; Dennis Lillee – 167; and Glenn McGrath – 157
5. Charles Bannerman at Sydney in the first Test of the 1886–7 series
6. Ray Illingworth, 1970–71 and 1972; and Mike Brearley, 1977–8 and 1979 – both with seven
7. 42 against England at Sydney in 1887–8
8. 18, between Melbourne in 1986–7 and The Oval in 1993
9. Ian and Greg Chappell in 1972, and Mark and Steve Waugh in 2001
10. Tom Richardson at Old Trafford – 1893, Lord's – 1896, Old Trafford – 1896, and Sydney – 1897–8
11. Clem Hill – 96, 97, 98, 98 and 99
12. John (J.J.) Warr
13. Jack Hobbs and Herbert Sutcliffe, Len Hutton and Cyril Washbrook (twice), and Geoffrey Boycott and John Edrich
14. George Gunn at Sydney in the second Test match of the 1886–7 series
15. Steve Waugh – 10
16. Edgbaston, Birmingham, in the second Test match of 2005; England won by 2 runs
17. Percy McDonnell of Australia in 1884 against England
18. F.S. 'Stanley' Jackson and Geoffrey Boycott
19. Clem Hill in the 1901–2 series
20. Rodney Marsh, when dismissing Bob Woolmer in the first Test match at Trent Bridge, Nottingham, in 1981

FOURS

1. Bill Ponsford and Doug Walters
2. Following the abandonment of the third Test match in Melbourne in 1970–71, the first ODI was played there on 5 January 1971 (a 40-over game)
3. Don Bradman, 103 not out, out of 191 at Melbourne during the 1932–3 series; and Colin Cowdrey, 102 out of 191 at Melbourne in the 1954–5 series
4. John Edrich

SIXES

1. Alastair Cook, Matt Prior and Andrew Strauss
2. Wayne Phillips

Miscellaneous 3

SINGLES

1. The 1986–7 series tour
2. (i) F.R. Spofforth at Melbourne – 1878–9, The Oval – 1882, Sydney – 1882–3, Sydney – 1884–5; (ii) Dennis Lillie at The Oval – 1972, Melbourne – 1976–7, Melbourne 1979–80, The Oval – 1981; (iii) Shane Warne at Brisbane – 1994–5, The Oval – 2001, Edgbaston – 2005, The Oval – 2005
3. W.A. 'Bertie' Oldfield – 31
4. David Gower
5. Allan Border – 29 occasions
6. A.C. 'Alick' Bannerman
7. Rodney Marsh
8. 1899
9. Colin Cowdrey
10. Trent Bridge, Nottingham
11. F.S. 'Stanley' Jackson (1905)
12. Adam Gilchrist in 2001, 2002–3 and 2006–7
13. Shane Warne and Dennis Lillee
14. Alec Stewart with 277 dismissals, including 36 as a fielder

15. Greg Chappell, who hit 108 against England at Perth in 1970–71, and 182 at Sydney in 1983–4
16. George Giffen
17. Wilfred Rhodes, who holds both the English partnership records for the first and tenth wicket
18. Shane Warne – 40 wickets, 249 runs and 5 catches, and Andrew Flintoff – 402 runs, 24 wickets and 3 catches
19. Clem Hill – 98 and 97 at Adelaide in 1901–2, and Frank Woolley – 95 and 93 at Lord's in 1921
20. Geraint Jones, born in Papua New Guinea

FOURS

1. F.R. 'Fred' Spofforth, 14 – 90 at The Oval in 1882, and R.A.L. 'Bob' Massie, 16 – 137 at the Lord's Test of 1972
2. John Barrett, Warren Bardsley, Bill Woodfull (twice), Bill Brown and Bill Lawry
3. George Lohmann of England – 112 wickets at 10.75 runs per wicket in 18 matches, achieving a record of 34 balls per dismissal in Test cricket
4. Derek Underwood and Alan Knott

SIXES

1. Ross Gregory
2. Peter Taylor – the New South Wales off-spinner

10   Trivia

Nicknames

SINGLES

1. Glenn McGrath
2. Ian Botham
3. Bill Lawry
4. Warwick Armstrong

5. Keith Miller
6. Darren Gough
7. A.N. Hornby
8. Ricky Ponting
9. G.J. 'George' Bonnor, who was 198 cm (6 ft 6 in.) tall
10. Justin Langer
11. 'Gelignite Jack'
12. Donald Bradman
13. W.M. 'Bill' Lawry
14. Colin Cowdrey
15. 'Tugga'
16. Robin Smith
17. Paul Reiffel
18. Marcus Trescothick
19. Mark Taylor
20. Jason Gillespie

FOURS

1. Frank Tyson
2. R.G.D. 'Bob' Willis
3. J.W.H.T. Douglas – England's captain in the 1911–12 and 1920–21 series
4. R. 'Bobby' Abel

SIXES

1. W.M. 'Bill' Woodfull
2. J.M. 'Jack' Blackham

Books and the Media
SINGLES

1. David Boon
2. Steve Waugh
3. Richie Benaud
4. Ian Botham
5. 1993

6. R.C. 'Jack' Russell
7. Jack Fingleton
8. Jim Laker
9. *Coming Back To Me*
10. Ian Botham
11. John Major
12. Dennis Lillee
13. Mike Brearley
14. Brett Lee
15. Graham Thorpe
16. Harold Larwood
17. Shane Warne
18. 1957
19. Nasser Hussain
20. Donald Bradman

FOURS

1. John Arlott
2. *Life, the Universe and Everything*, the third book of the *Hitchhiker's Guide to the Galaxy*
3. Fred Trueman
4. Douglas Jardine

SIXES

1. Steve Waugh
2. *The Final Test*

Pot Luck

SINGLES

1. George
2. Michael Angelow, who streaked at Lord's in 1975
3. Sir Pelham Warner
4. Sir Donald Bradman
5. Brisbane – the Woollongabba, to give its full title

6. D.B. 'Brian' Close aged 19 years and 301 days for the second Test at Melbourne in 1950–51
7. Adelaide
8. W.G. Grace, who was 50 years and 318 days old at Nottingham in 1899
9. 1891–2
10. Bowral, New South Wales
11. The Honourable I.F.W. 'Ivo' Bligh
12. Sydney Cricket Ground
13. Melbourne and Sydney with 53 Tests each
14. 1970–71; second Test match against England
15. 6 ft 8 in.
16. A.W. 'Tony' Greig at Brisbane in 1974–5 during the first Test, he was 6 ft 7 in. tall
17. Sheffield
18. The Lord's Museum
19. a) 1894–95
20. Sophia Gardens, Cardiff

FOURS

1. A batch of sub-standard balls kept going out of shape
2. Peru
3. Keith Miller
4. Barlow and Bates

SIXES

1. Hedley Verity
2. Ken Farnes

Acknowledgements

I would like to thank the staff at Hardie Grant, especially Clare Brenton for her support and encouragement, and for her help in getting the book before the public – she also seems to be on her way to becoming a cricket convert. Thanks also to Jane Aspden for commissioning the book, even though cricket isn't her strongest suit, and to Tom Whiting, Jane Beaton, Louise Harnby, Kate Pollard, Jessica Cuthbert-Smith and Vicky Newman for their assistance in getting the book to print.

I would also like to thank my daughter, Charlotte, for typing up the manuscript and deciphering my illegible scribble.

Acknowledgments